CW00693029

**Scene in the Author's garden. A boy learning to fire
from horseback**

Frontispiece

The
Complete Air-Gunner

by R. B. TOWNSHEND, M.A.

Member of the Legion of Frontiersmen,
Author of "Lone Pine", etc., etc.

WITH NUMEROUS ILLUSTRATIONS

*Including a series of Special Photographs
of the Cadet Corps of the*

STREATHAM GRAMMAR SCHOOL

ISBN 0 9507046 4 4

© HILLER AIRGUNS & PUBLICATIONS, 1984
56, Princess Way, Euxton, Chorley, Lancs.

CONTENTS

LIST OF ILLUSTRATIONS

AIR-GUN TARGETS.

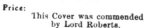

PREFACE.

THE object of this book is to put forward a few ideas on home culture in rifle shooting. The literature of club rifle shooting now covers a very wide field, and it would be natural to imagine that no single section of the sport had been overlooked. Yet though many excellent works have already been published, they leave as a rule the impression that practice can only be obtained with the help of some kind of elaborate club organisation, involving the provision of a special ground and of a somewhat costly equipment. The author has, however, found that an ordinary garden can be readily fitted up as a rifle range without danger or nuisance to the neighbours, and that it is possible within its limits to give instruction of real value in all the essentials of marksmanship. This end is achieved by the use of a weapon which has only of late years received the attention of skilled manufacturers. The modern air-rifle is decidedly a weapon of precision. Its ballistics—if so high-sounding a name may be used in such a connection—are, nevertheless so low that no danger need be apprehended when a proper system of bullet-catcher is employed. It has been the author's pleasure for many years past to diversify the exercise of marksmanship under ordinary range conditions with garden practice, using first the air-gun, and later on the improved model of air-rifle. Not only has the air-rifle given him many enjoyable hours of practice, but it has been the means of arousing in the sons of many among his friends a keen interest in rifle shooting and enabling them to get some acquaintance with the theory involved. He has amused himself by devising targets of several different kinds in order that the change from one to the other may relieve the monotony of always shooting at the same mark in the same way. Snap-shooting, for instance, affords a pleasant variety, but as it necessarily involves less precision of aim than is possible at a stationary mark, the air-rifle with its light bullet and low velocity becomes particularly well adapted for the work, because stray shots can be caught against any natural background, so that even if an occasional pellet misses the target no trouble need be apprehended. The apparatus of the garden air-rifle club may accordingly include a running-man range, as well as a fairly realistic representation of a galloping horse, from which useful shooting practice can be obtained. These and all other matters dealt with in the present volume have been worked out by the author under practical conditions, without for a moment anticipating that material suitable for a book would be evolved. As time went on it became apparent that miniature rifle clubs, wide as they now spread their nets, cannot bring shooting within the reach of everybody. The author's method of employing the air-rifle in combination with a garden rifle range began to assume a more and more practical bearing on one of the most urgent problems of the day. The writing of the present volume was accordingly undertaken, and he has heartily enjoyed setting out in systematised form various improvements and ideas which have been developed during recent years, while he has also been able to draw on his earlier shooting experiences on the Great Plains and in the Rocky Mountains.

The Complete Air-Gunner.

CHAPTER I

Drawing a Bead.

THE heart's desire of every right-minded boy is to prove himself a man, and he is secretly convinced that the first quality of a man is to be a warrior. Our boys have inherited this conviction from very far back. It dates from many hundreds of generations ago—perhaps from many thousands. In the early struggles of mankind for existence the first thing needful, alike for the tribe and the individual, was the power of self-defence. For this two things are requisite above all else—one a virtue, the other an art. The virtue is courage; the art is the mastery of arms. Every savage must still possess those two, though we citizens of a civilised State need not, so long as Private Atkins and Policeman X have them for us. But the wise boy prefers to have them himself, and he is right.

There is much that the boy does for himself. He learns courage naturally, in the society of his fellows, in the free life of the playground, the school, and the street. But the mastery of arms—nay, even the use of the naked hands—will not come to him from Nature, but by teaching. And we older men, if we are wise, will see that the boy gets the teaching.

Well I remember how, more than thirty years ago, before the buffalo were killed off, I spent a winter in the village of a Red Indian tribe. When I arrived, the young men were absent—gone off, all of them, on a buffalo hunt. In a few days they returned, their horses loaded down with meat and with buffalo hides. And they proudly pointed out to me a boy—a handsome, bright-eyed young redskin of fifteen. "That is the best boy," they told me. "He rode his pony up alongside a great bull buffalo, and drove home that lance there between the ribs to the vitals." And at the praise the warm blood mantled in the young warrior's cheek to a modest blush.

These Indians still stuck to the bow and the spear— the ancient weapons of their race—and they knew well how to use them. Bow and spear and sword are the weapons of antiquity and of romance. Israelites and Philistines slew each other thus, and with them the war of Greeks and Trojans was decided. To-day if those Indians were to go buffalo-hunting (alas! there are now no buffalo to hunt), they would carry guns. To-day the bow and spear and sword find their place only in the museum. Men who go to hunt or to make war must have rifles and cannon. There is nothing else in it. The soldier of the line with his rifle, the artilleryman with his field-guns and his siege-train—they are the warriors of to-day.

Rifles and cannon have ousted the others because, thanks to modern improvements, we now kill men a hundred times further off and a hundred times more surely than with the weapons of old—at least, we do so when our hands and our eyes are trained to use them rightly. There is the crux. The rifle must be held straight, or the man behind the gun might as well be shooting peas out of a peashooter. There is a man in the British Army who in one minute has fired forty shots with the Service arm—the ordinary rifle carried by the linesman—and at one hundred yards he hit the bull's-eye thirty-nine times. Take a man who had never learned to shoot, and he probably would not get off five shots in the minute, nor hit a haystack with any one of them. We cannot all be champion shots; but any man with sound eyes and steady nerves can make himself an effective rifleman, fit as far as shooting is concerned to take his place in the line alongside of the British soldier. It is fortunate for England, apt to put things off as she is, that the rifle can be learned quicker than the bow. Six months will now make a marksman. It took six years to make an archer, and the archer had to learn as a child to "lay his body to the bow" if he was ever to become really effective. The art of shooting may be acquired in middle life; but, like all other bodily arts, it is best and easiest mastered in youth.

Nor in this matter is there any distinction to be drawn between cannon and rifle. Both must be aimed straight at the mark if they are to do any good, and in both the movements gone through in laying them straight are controlled by the eye of a man looking along the sights. So the first thing in shooting is to learn to use the sights, or, as the frontiersman calls it, to draw a bead. Let us take a rifle in our hands, and for this purpose any rifle will do, be it a miniature weapon weighing some four or five pounds, a military weapon weighing nine or ten, or one of the old elephant-guns that may

be twice as heavy again. Whichever it may be, you will
see two projections above the barrel—one near the muzzle
and one near the breech—which are known as the fore-
sight and the back-sight respectively. They lie more or less
·in line with the axis of the barrel, and when these sights,
looked at from behind, are seen to point at the centre
of the target the barrel-axis should point at an imaginary
vertical line drawn through the bull's-eye. Then, if the
trigger is pressed, supposing that the rifle is loaded and
cocked, the explosion of the powder should propel the
bullet forwards so that it strikes that line. That is all
there is to it—a steel tube, a pinch of powder, a half-
ounce of lead, two sights, and the man behind the gun.
Yet it has taken "villainous saltpetre" a good many
centuries to oust the cold steel that our ancestors gloried
in.

Let us consider the sights—the
two little excrescences on the tube,
without which all the rest are as naught.
The one near the muzzle is the fore-
sight. Looked at from behind, it will appear either as
a bead or as a cone or barleycorn. The latter is more
 often found in military weapons, the
former in sporting ones. There are
other forms, but these two are good
enough for most men.
The sight near the breech is the
back-sight. You will see that it has a flat top with a
nick in the middle, or perhaps there is no nick or notch,
but instead a vertical white line in the middle of the
upright face. As before, there are other forms ; but these
are the commonest, and are good enough. They will do
their business, and that business is to kill. An ounce of

lead can finish off the best man, or the worst, when the sights are straight.

I remember once looking at the cockpit of the *Victory* with a British admiral, and a little thing he said stuck in my mind. It was, " Many a brave man—*and many a coward*—died here." So one might say of the sights of a rifle, " Many a brave man—and many a coward—has taken his last look at the world up the sights of a rifle—seen the wrong way."

And here I would lay down as the very first maxim for everyone, be it man or boy or woman, who handles arms, " Never point a gun or allow a gun to be pointed at anyone either in joke or through carelessness. If you see it being done, do not hesitate to stop it." Nor is the miserable excuse, " Oh, it isn't loaded! " to be tolerated. The person at whom the gun points does not *know* it isn't loaded, and the one who points it does not always know it either. If this rule were obeyed, the " accidental death " rate would fall considerably.

Now to return to our bead-drawing. Take a piece of black paper, and cut out a pattern shaped like the fore-sight of your weapon, be it bead or barleycorn. Also cut out another piece like the back-sight, with its notch or nick in the middle. Now make a round dot on a piece of white paper to represent the bull's-eye, and arrange your two pieces of black paper beneath it like this : That is how the sights are to appear to the eye when you look down the rifle at the target. The top of the bead or barleycorn should not encroach on the bull—it should not even quite touch it—but there should be a very small space of white visible between the two.

Move your paper sights about a little at a time, and see what variations you can make in drawing a bead. The fore-sight can appear in the notch to the right, or to the left, or central. Central, of course, is right for normal shooting; but you may find it convenient sometimes to draw your bead a little to one side. Again, you can choose to see either much or little of the fore-sight in the notch. If it is level with the top of the notch thus, it is called *full;*

if above the notch thus, *very full;*

if only the tip remains visible, it is a *fine* sight.

Remember these four things :—

A fine sight makes the bullet strike lower.

A full sight makes it strike higher.

The fore-sight seen in the right of the notch makes it strike to the right.

The fore-sight seen in the left of the notch makes it strike to the left.

It is a good plan to cut out for yourself various patterns of back-sights—wide V's, shallow V's, narrow V's, deep V's, and try them all. There is a large choice in this matter when you come to shoot, and each man has a right to his own taste.

There is an excellent device called Christie's Aiming Card, sold for 3d. by the dealers in the many articles

PLATE II

"The sights of a rifle—seen the wrong way"

that shooting men like to possess, on which a bull's-eye and a movable pair of cardboard sights are cleverly arranged so that any desired way of aligning them can be shown.   I have found it very useful in teaching beginners at the start, and also in reminding them of how they can vary their sighting afterwards.

Now to try drawing a bead with the rifle itself.   Take a table and chair, indoors or out, and on the table put something for the rifle to rest upon.   For myself I prefer to build a solid, substantial support, in the shape of a wooden rest like a four-legged stool, a foot long, a foot high, and nine inches wide.   The top is not flat, but V-shaped, three inches lower in the middle than the sides, and it may have a pair of pads, made of any common fabric and stuffed with shavings, which are to be tied or tacked, one to each slope, so that the rifle will rest easily and securely in the hollow between them.   But if this is too much trouble, it is a simple matter to build up an impromptu rest out of a few big books, or boards, and cushions.

Hang on the opposite wall, at a convenient height, a target with a bull's-eye that you can see comfortably— say half an inch in diameter.   Sit down on the chair, support your elbows on the table, put the rifle on the rest, and align it so that the top of the fore-sight is visible in the notch just below the bull, just as you did with the cardboard sights.   Compare your impression now with the way the cardboard sights looked.   Then you saw all three things—back-sight, fore-sight, and bull—equally sharp, because they were practically at the same distance from the eye.   But now they are all at different distances, and you will find that you cannot get all three sharply defined.   Look direct at the back-sight.   You see it sharp enough ; but your eye is now focussed on an object hardly a foot away, and you will perceive that the fore-sight is comparatively dim, while as for the bull you almost lose it altogether. Now look direct at the fore-sight, and you will perceive that the edges of the notch in the back-sight, and, indeed, all its outlines, are slightly blurred and hazy. The bull, however, has become much clearer. That is because the eye is focussed for a distance at least twice or thrice as great as when you looked direct at the back-sight.

Now leaving the rifle on the rest, pointed as before, draw your head back a couple of feet, and you will find that you are able to see the three things much sharper. But it would be impossible to bring to the shoulder a rifle with a stock a couple of feet longer than at present, neither would it be possible to put the back-sight a couple of feet forward, because then it would be right up against the fore-sight, unless you also made the barrel two feet longer, so as to put the fore-sight forward. That would mean a four or five foot barrel. In our museums you may see arms from India and Africa with barrels five feet long and even more. They use them in Morocco to-day, but we do not go to Morocco for patterns. The museum is the proper place for such weapons.

At present the best we can do is to apologise for the deficiencies of the human eye, stick to a rifle fitted with a barrel not over thirty inches long, and shoot as well as we are able with a back-sight that is bound to be some-what blurred. It is a compromise, like most other human arrangements ; but, considering the number of bulls a good shot will put on at a thousand yards, we must admit that it is one that works well.

Neither is the imperfection of the human eye the sole

difficulty in the matter of drawing a bead.   Hold the
rifle on the bull's-eye and consider the sights.   They
shake visibly.   See if you can detect a rhythm in the
shaking.   Listen to your heart beating, if you can, or
observe the throbs of your pulse.   The sights shake in
time with it.   Unless you can stop your heart beating,
you cannot hold the sights perfectly still—not even now
when you are sitting calmly in a chair in your quiet house
or garden, with your pulse presumably beating between
sixty and seventy.   Suppose you had been running as
hard as you could go after a bear (or with the bear after
you), at what rate would your pulse be going?   Probably
a hundred or a hundred and ten, and thumping like an
engine.   Your best chance then is to catch a rapid sight
between the throbs—if you can.

Nor is a man's pulse the only thing that causes his
hand to shake.   We all have nerves, and drink and fury
and fear, not to speak of other matters, are liable to
upset them.   Who does not know how hard the nerves
are to control?   What golfer has never missed a short
putt?   Did not Henry of Navarre shake visibly as he
rode into the fight at Ivry, when his heroic soul flung at
his trembling body that grimmest of sardonic jests, " If
you only knew where I am presently going to take you,
you would tremble twice as much."   Truly it is not so
simple a matter to draw a bead.

CHAPTER II.

Position in Shooting.

Now that we know what drawing a bead is, let us proceed to try the various positions in which we can shoot, and note the effects. There are at least five regular positions—standing, sitting, kneeling, lying prone, and lying on the back, and these are exemplified in the various Plates. You may try all these either indoors or out, and by lamplight as well as by daylight. Take a good-sized mirror and set it up some five feet from the ground, and if you are indoors let it be placed so that the light falls on it suitably.

Take your stand opposite to it with the rifle in your hands, the right hand on the grip or small of the stock, the left a little in front of the trigger guard. Face half right with the left foot forward, as you see the boys standing in Plate III.; raise the rifle, bringing the butt well in to the shoulder, and take aim at your own face in the glass. Keep both eyes open, let your right eye see the top of the fore-sight in the notch of the back-sight, and point the rifle so that the sights bear on the mark; let the mark be the middle of your face between the eyebrows. Do this correctly, and you have " drawn

PLATE III

a bead " on your other self, who, you will observe, is pointing his rifle straight on you.

Now close the left eye, and without moving the rifle verify with the right eye whether you were holding the sights on the mark. If you find that they were quite off it, change your hands on the rifle so that you put the left on the grip and the right in front of the trigger guard, face round half left, and bring the rifle to the left shoulder. Draw a bead on yourself, as before, with both eyes open, only allow the left eye to do the work of bringing the sights into line on the mark. If now you find it easy to get the sights true with your left eye when you have both eyes open, it may mean that your left eye is the predominant partner, that it is the " master eye " in fact, and that it will be an advantage to you to become a left-shoulder shot. If the quality of vision in the right eye is known to be equal to that of the left, the tendency to align with the left eye arises from inability to control the impressions passing from the eyes to the brain. With healthy eyes the nerves soon accustom themselves to signal to the brain the image which impresses itself on the eye looking along the sight.

But whichever eye may be the stronger it is worth while to be able to shoot at will from either shoulder. The accident of a wound disabling one eye need not put out of action the man who shoots with his right or left indifferently, while for horseback work it is invaluable, because in the saddle it is hardly possible to shoot with the right eye at anything on your right-hand side. There is a very ancient story of the sailorman and the parson, where the seagoer had the best of the preacher because the latter could only say his prayers forwards, while the sailor boxed his compass both ways, forwards and back.

Let the man who wishes to be truly master of his weapon learn to be, like the sailor, familiar with it both ways.

Assuming, however, that your eyes are normal, let us go on with right-shoulder shooting. Draw a bead on your counterfeit in the glass, and then close the left eye. Note if doing this makes you crease your forehead and pucker your eyebrows. If you are doing so, you will in all probability also find that the right eyelid is trying to close of itself, by force of sympathy, and is thus obstructing the vision of the eye. You should overcome this by practising until you can " wink the other eye " without interfering in the least with the open one. Your object is to be able to shoot with either eye closed or with both open without conscious effort. At the targets you must be free to concentrate all your attention on the aim, and not have to worry about controlling your facial muscles. This will not be accomplished till you can draw a bead on the image in the glass without making wry faces over it.

Next look again at Plate III., and consider the position of your head. You should hold it well up, not canted far over to the right or squeezed down to the stock of the rifle. Stand erect, and raise the right elbow as high as the right shoulder. That will bring the shoulder up to the head instead of lowering the head to the shoulder. Let the left elbow come well forward, and almost vertically under the rifle. For deliberate shooting this is the best position ; when a man shoots at birds on the wing with a shot-gun his right elbow is not so high and his left not so low, and when you come to try quick shots at the running deer you will probably hold your arms as he does. It is well to practise both ways, but in either case hold up your head.

Let your weight rest about equally on both your feet, which may be some fifteen inches apart, the left in advance, and both pointing somewhere about half right, but the left rather the less of the two. If you play golf it may interest you to observe that the position very nearly resembles the " stance " adopted for the drive by a golfer who stands " open." But be careful not to cramp yourself at all in taking up your stance, to use the convenient golfing term. " Always make yourself comfortable " is a good maxim for shooting. Find out by experiment just how you want to place yourself, so that you feel steadiest and best able to control the movements of your weapon. That is for you the best " stance " possible.

Now, with the rifle at the shoulder, swing your body round on your hips, letting the rifle cover as wide a horizontal sweep as it can. You will find that you are able to cover something like a semicircle without shifting your feet. When you are at the running man or deer you have to swing the rifle round, following the movement of the mark, and you must stand steady in order to do this rightly. Again, bend the body back till the rifle points straight overhead. You are now in the position for shooting a rook at the top of a high tree. Bend forward and aim in front of your toes, and you have the position for firing, it may be at a seal or a mountain sheep, over the edge of a precipice. You will see that standing up offers you an extraordinary variety of possible shots, far more than any other position.

Next, to try the sitting position, take a stool about nine inches high, and put the glass on the ground and the stool opposite to it, but turned so that it faces 45 deg. to the right. Sit down on it, and extend your feet so that the left knee points nearly straight to the glass, with the right knee almost at right angles.   Lean a little forward, and rest the elbows on the knees, and aim at your counterfeit presentment once more, shifting yourself till you are thoroughly at your ease.   You may observe the gain in steadiness from the support the knees give to the elbows.   You may also notice that instead of the freedom of swing which you had when standing up, you now can hardly aim off the glass without shifting your seat. But take your right elbow off the knee and swing, and you will find much more freedom.   You can now swing so as to traverse perhaps from the eighth to the sixth part of a circle.   This comparative freedom when the right elbow is loose makes the sitting position a useful one to the game shot.   At Bisley men often use it at the running deer. Also you notice that your eyes are high enough above the ground to enable you to shoot over the top of tolerably long grass, which you can hardly do lying down.

The kneeling position is not much used now, since mounted infantry and spurs came in.   You can easily try it by removing the stool and sitting on your right heel instead, for which purpose it is advisable to wear a heavy boot with a strong stiff sole.   In this position the eyes are at about the same height as if you were sitting on a bank a foot high.   To get the eyes a few inches higher you may half rise, standing as it were on the right knee, but still keeping the elbow resting on the left.   In this position you could shoot over high mowing grass.

Lastly, we come to the two lying-down positions, one prone and the other lying on the back.   The prone is the position almost universally used at present, for two reasons.   One is that men who are creeping forward, whether in battle or after game, and keeping their bodies

PLATE IV

as much under cover as possible, naturally drop forward whenever they stop, and so are already in the prone position to shoot. The other is that when you rest the elbows on the ground you can take a steadier shot. In order to try it, lie down before the glass, not straight, but facing exactly as you did when sitting, that is to say, about 45 deg. to the right. As you look in the glass you should see your left leg extended well away to the left, as in Plates V. and IX. Some men keep both legs nearly together, but the orthodox position, as shown in the Plates, is to widen the angle between them till the feet are spread something like forty-eight inches, and the shooter lies with the toes pointing out, heels flat to the ground.

Lie as comfortably as you can, and fit your rifle butt in snugly to your shoulder. Let the left elbow come well to the front and rest nearly under the rifle barrel, with the right elbow somewhat behind it, so that when you look in the glass there is no great distance apparently between the two elbows. This position, with the right shoulder well back, minimises the shock of the recoil when you come to fire a heavy rifle with the full charge. With a small rifle there is practically no recoil, but you may as well get accustomed to the best position for the other. Let your head be as high as it conveniently can, with the chest and shoulders well raised. You want the chest to be able to expand freely, and to give play to the lungs. The prone position is somewhat cramping, and unless you can breathe well you will find it hard to keep your aim steady. Watch the shoulders of your reflection; you will see them rise as you fill the lungs. Breathe deeply once or twice; then exhale slowly, shut the mouth, and hold the breath. Then for a couple of seconds you can remain almost absolutely still. This when you shoot is the moment to choose for loosing off.

Lastly try the back position. Seat yourself on the ground facing the glass; cross the ankles, with the left above, and place the rifle barrel in the angle between them; lie down on the back, turning a little on the right side, and draw the butt into the armpit. The right hand grasps the rifle by the grip as usual, but the left either rests on top of the butt and steadies it in to the shoulder, or else it is placed behind the neck and supports the head. Lying on the back with the head elevated is very trying to the neck, unless you put your hand there or clench a wrist strap in the teeth, as in Plate XVI. So strained and unnatural does this very odd attitude seem at first that you will be apt to find it ridiculous. Nevertheless, it is the steadiest of all positions when you are used to it. You will notice that the sights are so far from the eye that it is hard to adjust them well. This is one of the reasons why the back position is accounted unmilitary, and is rarely seen at Bisley, except in special competitions for match rifles. Men who shoot in these have a special sight fitted very far back on the rifle stock, so as to be close to the eye. An air-rifle fitted with this sight is shown in Plate XIII. Most men who use the position lay the right knee nearly flat on the ground, and rest the gun on the right thigh and calf, with the left leg nearly upright from the knee downwards.* And there are even some who lie quite on the right side, with both knees together and the barrel resting on the outside of the left thigh. Try all these in turn, and you will be surprised at the acrobatic feats that are demanded of you.

---

* The shooter depicted in Plate XIII. shoots from the left shoulder, so that right becomes left and *vice versâ*.

PLATE V

" A man might as well try to shoot standing on his head," you say.

So he might. I have seen a man in a show shoot standing on his head, and do it very well too.

" What's the use of such a thing?" you ask.

Possibly none in itself, but there is a great deal of use in being able to use your weapon no matter how awkward and constrained the position in which you find yourself. Let me give an instance.

A sheep-owner not far from my ranch tried to run a buffalo bull on a mare that had never seen a buffalo. Horses have a great natural terror of buffalo, and the mare gave such a wild jump sideways when the buffalo turned that the sheepman fell off. The buffalo charged him, and he, still prostrate, managed to lay the rifle across his left thigh as he lay on his right side, and had the good fortune to disable his dangerous antagonist. It was truly a lucky hit for him, for he shot as badly as he rode, and he had certainly never before tried the experiment of lying on his side and firing over the thigh. Yet, here, this position, ridiculous as it looks, whether you see it at Bisley or on your drawing-room floor, was just what was wanted.

Let me give you a second instance of what one may call a fancy position being practically useful. So far we have been aiming with the head erect and the sights upright. But it is quite possible to aim either a rifle or a pistol with the head on one side and the sights horizontal instead of vertical. You could not hit anything that way at a long range, because the bullet would not fly straight, but it can go true enough at close quarters.

This thing happened out in the Far West. A settler

whom I knew there had a certain enemy, who came up to him one day quite suddenly, put a derringer to his breast, and shot him right through.   His enemy, thinking he had satisfactorily finished him, walked quickly away. The victim, though desperately wounded, was not finished : he got out his own pistol and, aiming with it held sideways as he lay all twisted up on the ground, shot his would-be murderer stone dead.   He had never tried a shot like that before, so he told us afterwards, but it is one you may see performed in any show, being, as it is, a well-recognised form of trick shot, and not a difficult one.

I remember a somewhat similar duel which was decided, not by a trick shot, but by a rapid adjustment to the circumstances.   In 1872 or 1873 a young cavalry officer in the United States Army met, quite unexpectedly, an enemy of his at close quarters on the steps of the Planters' House, in Louisville, Kentucky.   Both men drew and fired hurriedly ; both missed, and then lost sight of each other in the cloud of smoke which the black powder of those days gave off.   But smoke always rises.   Forgetful of this, the officer still remained standing ; his wiser enemy, dropping on his left hand and knee, got under the smoke, took a sure aim, and poor Captain A. fell.   The survivor had thought out his combinations beforehand, and was able to put them in practice at the critical moment.

Again, take this instance.   There is a well-known form of trick shot by which you look in a glass and shoot by making the reflection of your weapon point straight at the reflection of the mark you desire to hit.   One time when I was in Denver a man was sitting in the back of a shop, and there he suddenly saw reflected in the

PLATE VI

glass of the show-case his deadly enemy entering the door.   He did not turn his head, but quietly drew out his pistol, waited till his unconscious foe came close behind him, aimed his pistol, by means of the glass, over his left shoulder, fired backwards, and got his man.

I tell these cruel stories—for it is a cruel thing that man should slay his brother man—not for the sake of the horror they rouse, but to emphasise the fact that when you are suddenly "up against it" you may find the conditions novel, and short indeed the time in which to adapt yourself.   As I look back and think over these things (and many more like them) it seems to me that no one can be too familiar with the use of his weapon under every possible combination of circumstances.   The survivor in the long run is he who is master of arms.

CHAPTER III.

Air-Guns of the Past.

FOR learning how to draw a bead, practically any rifle will do; but now when we come to firing at a mark the question of what arm to begin with arises. Certainly we will not take the $:303$ Service rifle. Let me say, in parenthesis, that the diameter of the bore, or calibre, of a rifle is commonly expressed in decimals of an inch. For instance, the Service rifle is known as the $\cdot 303$, because it has a calibre of $\frac{303}{1000}$, or nearly one-third, of an inch. The Snider had one of $\cdot 577$, or over half an inch. This odd sounding figure is explainable by the circumstance that $\cdot 577$ is the diameter of a spherical ball running 24 to the pound. One hears of 4-bore rifles and 8-bores, the $\cdot 577$ is based on the 24-bore. The more recent calibres, since the Snider, have not been based on round-ball sizes. The popular little $\cdot 22$ rifles, whose name is legion, have a diameter of bore between one-quarter and one-fifth of an inch. The reason for not beginning with a $:577$ or a $\cdot 303$ is that weapons like these when fired with a full charge make a loud noise and give a hard kick. Now it is all-important to acquire the habit of not flinching when you press the trigger, so that it is far better to begin with a rifle that does neither, such as the air-gun, or the little ·22, the Morris Tube, or the Service rifle fitted with a ·22 calibre barrel. The Morris Tube is a small rifle-barrel, which can be slipped inside the ·303 or any other larger barrel fitted for it, and can then be fired with a small cartridge of its own. But though the tube and the ·22 have no kick and little report, they must none the less be treated as deadly weapons. Both are capable of killing a man at 100 or 200 yards. Consequently they should only be used where a safe range of considerable length is available. Here is where the air-gun and air-rifle have an advantage. The art of shooting may be thoroughly learnt with them, and yet, with the exercise of due care, they may safely be used in a room or a garden. Let me emphasise " with care." Any weapon is dangerous in the hands of an idiot, even the umbrella with which he carelessly pokes out your eye.

Nor is its comparative safety the only advantage of the air-gun. It is also clean. " Villainous saltpetre " has a smell which is not welcomed in the house or even in the garden, besides which it fouls the barrel so that after use the bore must be thoroughly cleansed. The charm of the air-gun is that you may fire a thousand shots down its barrel, and all it asks for is a drop of oil.

The air-gun, like some other charming things, has a past. In the middle of the last century it was constructed with a big metal bulb, externally attached, or else with a hollow stock of steel, to act as a reservoir for the compressed air which was forced into it with a pump, just as it is to-day into the tyres of a motor-car. This involved violent exertion, even on the part of the strongest man. Then a bullet, or a charge of shot, was placed in the chamber, and when the trigger was pressed the hammer struck the face of a valve and released a proper amount of the store of compressed air, which rushed down the barrel, driving the charge before it. The process could be repeated as long as the pressure of the air in the reservoir was high enough, and this usually lasted for six or seven shots. Air-guns of this type enjoyed a certain vogue in those early days among poachers on account of their silence and the celerity with which their half-dozen shots could be fired; however, they never attained great popularity, partly because of their high cost, and partly on account of the severe labour of charging, which even then failed to produce substantial uniformity of result over a series of rounds. That nothing is new under the sun is curiously exemplified by the fact that the rotating breech-plug of the modern air-rifle exactly reproduces the system of breech-closure as used in these air-rifles of fifty years ago.

An entirely new set of conditions was introduced when the smooth-bore air-gun known as the " Gem " was first placed on the market. This gun was a marvel of ingenious design; but, although it became very popular, it suffered from the serious defect that it was made up rather as a toy than as a practical gun, and the immense strength of its propelling-spring produced a strain on the parts which they were not strong enough to stand. Although it sold in thousands and tens of thousands, it earned the reputation of quickly going wrong; in fact, these air-guns frequently became unserviceable after a few days' use. The chief cause of trouble was the overloading of the propelling-spring, and the severe strain on the piston-releasing mechanism working in conjunction with the trigger. No one, in fact, but a clever mechanic could keep one of the early type of air-guns in a constant

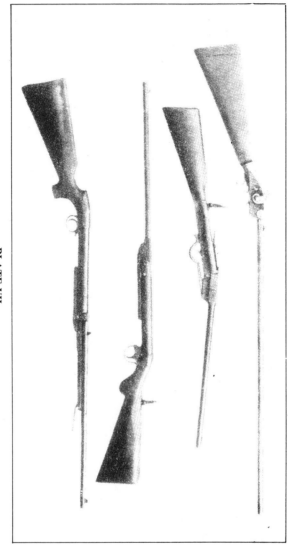

PLATE VII

An ancient Air-Rifle with reservoir in the butt.

Hinged Barrel pattern of spring Air-Gun.

"Millita" style of the same (Greener-Lane pattern).

B.S.A. model with separate cocking lever and rifled barrel.

state of efficient repair. The piston was always slipping from its supports at a critical moment in the loading operation, with the result that the connecting-link received a severe blow which put most of the parts out of gear.

Whatever may have been its faults of construction, the " Gem " air-gun represented an originality of purpose and an ingenuity of design which entitle it to rank amongst the noteworthy inventions of the last century. Yet manufacturers were slow to appreciate the underlying merits of a weapon which they too readily condemned because of defects that a careful examination would have shown to be due to bad manufacture. The essential novelty of the spring system of air-gun was that the air was used immediately it had been compressed. Now a large part of the energy which is used in compressing air in a reservoir shows itself in the form of heat. In time the surplus heat is dissipated, and the original pressure is much reduced. This loss of temperature represents a serious waste of energy expended in pumping. Hence there is a great loss of efficiency in any system of air-gun construction which involves compressing the air before it is wanted. In the spring air-gun little or no heat is lost, because the power is stored in the form of spring-compression, and the air is not compressed until the exact moment when it is to be used. This additional source of efficiency, combined with a diminution of bore and bullet weight, made it possible to produce practical shooting results with only the slight physical effort which is involved in setting a spring by means of suitably-arranged levers.

The system of leverage employed in the original air-gun had one very grave disadvantage. The lever consisted of the barrel itself, which was pivoted on a

hinge at the breech for the purpose. Every time the
force of a man's arm was applied to the barrel-lever to
compress the propelling-spring it was necessarily subjected
to a severe bending strain. Now, properly hardened
spring steel will bear a considerable strain and return
again to its original shape, but rifle-barrels are made with
other ends in view, and the slightest pressure on the barrel
will alter the direction of the shooting. The violent
treatment involved in using the barrel as a cocking-lever
is, therefore, inadmissible.

Nor is the unfair strain to which the barrel-lever is
subjected the only, perhaps I should say the main,
objection to be made to this system of loading an air-gun.
Unless certain precautions are observed the man who
handles it may suffer injury as well as the mechanism,
and ignorance of this fact may lead to serious mischief.
After the spring has been compressed, but before the
barrel has been returned to its original position, the
weapon is like a set rat-trap. If the trigger be
accidentally released, or if the catch where it engages
with the piston should slip, the spring instantly drives
the piston forward, and the barrel flies up to its first
position with great violence. Now, if your finger and
thumb are in the opening of the breech, as they must be
in order to put the slug in the chamber, or if you are
holding the gun with a finger, or fingers, underneath the
grip, you will inevitably get pinched by the violent closing
of the action. I am glad to say that in all these years
I have never had a serious accident to anyone shooting
with my air-guns, and I have often had a dozen going
at once; but I have heard of such a thing happening,
and I am quite sure one cannot be too careful.

This danger can, and should, be avoided by loading

in the position shown in Plate XI. After the spring has been compressed the gun should be held, as shown, with the stock under the armpit and the barrel firmly grasped in the hand not far from the muzzle. If the spring were now accidentally released, the armpit holds down the stock, while the firm hand-grasp is sufficient to keep the barrel from flying up and closing, and, therefore, the fingers of the other hand which are putting the slug into the chamber would escape being nipped. My advice is that this precaution should never be neglected in loading any air-gun in which the barrel opens at the breech.

CHAPTER IV.

The Gun of the Future.

IT was not until air-gun shooting became a favourite social amusement in workmen's clubs in the Midlands that a serious effort was made to diminish the more objectionable mechanical defects of existing weapons. Air-guns constantly came back for repair; indeed, a single gunsmith in Birmingham kept three men in his shop employed merely in mending breakdowns; and this led to improvements designed to obviate these irritating mishaps. The competitive aspects of club shooting also produced a demand for enhanced accuracy, and the net result was that a new type was designed which was put on the market some years ago under the title of the Millita. In the earlier air gun one defect was that the propelling spring was set far back towards the butt in the grip of the stock, which, of course, necessarily lies at a considerable angle with the barrel. When the gun was fired, the push of the spring and the blow of the piston on the head of the cylinder were delivered not in a straight line with the barrel, but at an angle from below. This tended to disturb the alignment. In the Millíta this particular difficulty was overcome by lengthening the whole arm considerably, as may be seen from Plate VII., which shows a Millita air-gun. This increase of length allowed the main working parts, namely, the cylinder, piston, and spring, to be removed from the butt and the grip of the gun and put further forward where the hinge of the barrel had formerly been, and the hinge in its turn was put several inches further on in front of them. But the barrel was still utilised as a lever to compress the spring, so that the mechanical principle remained the same as in the early type. Now, however, the striking parts of the action being in the same line as the barrel, the shock of the discharge disturbed the alignment less, and the gun shot better. But the rifled air-gun was still to come.

Rifling itself, of course, is nothing new. For nearly three centuries it has been known that by grooving a barrel so as to make the bullet spin it was quite practicable to ensure far greater accuracy in the bullet's course. The difficulty with the air-gun had been that the twisted grooves of the rifling added so much to the friction that the bullet having only a low velocity often stuck fast in the barrel. Experiments also had been made with a view to getting a spin in smooth-bored air-guns by means of slugs of elongated shape having twisted flanges cast or impressed on them; their spin, however, could not always be depended upon. Beyond a certain range, which in my experience usually proves to be about eight yards, but naturally varies with the velocity and weight of the slugs, you will find that a large proportion of non-spinning bullets " keyhole "; that is to say, they turn over in the air and strike up against the target sideways, making a hole in the paper in shape not unlike the keyhole of a door. The object of concentrating the weight of an air-gun slug forward is that the attenuated rear shall act as the feathers on an arrow, and so keep the slug travelling end on. Every practical shot knows that unless bullets do that there is no depending on their accuracy. The object of rifling is to keep the bullet spinning round its axis, point forward, and you can get some idea of the quality of the shooting you may expect from a rifle by the clean circular perforations its bullets make.

Various patterns of slugs are still manufactured in order to get as good shooting as possible from smooth-bore guns. Some have a circular flange at the base, and others have a hollow base which can be expanded so as to fit the barrel tightly enough, yet not too tight. The object is to take the rifling, if the gun is rifled, and in any case to give the bullet an air-tight fit in the barrel. Obviously if any air escapes past the bullet in the barrel, so much force is lost. Experience seems to prove that the best results with rifled barrels are obtained by a slug in the form of two truncated cones joined together, with the bases away from each other, and a cup in the rear end. Such a slug lies evenly in the barrel, touching it only at front and back, thus causing the minimum of friction, while, the forward end being heavier, the slug has less tendency to turn over in its flight. Shot from a good air-rifle such a slug is quite capable of keeping its axis true for a hundred yards, and can be confidently relied upon to do so for twenty. Even in smooth-bored air-guns I have satisfied myself by experiment that with these slugs decidedly more regular shooting can be obtained than with any flanged or expanded slugs that I have used.

One system of a different sort may be mentioned here. The Quackenbush Combination air-rifle, ·22 calibre, made in America, when used with ordinary slugs does not in my experience shoot better than other hinged-barrel guns, nor indeed as well as some. But if it be used with the felted 21½—100 slugs specially made for it, I find that it shoots very true up to ten or twelve yards. The barrel is beautifully rifled, and a felt wad is stuck on to the base of the slug a trifle larger than the bore. When the gun is fired, the slug can pass freely down without taking the grooves, but the thick felt takes them and imparts the spin. The objection to the system is its cost. These felted slugs, which are between sizes 3 and 2, cost 5s. per 1000, or half as much as ·22 rim fire cartridges, compared with 9d. to 1s. 6d. per 1000 for the different makes of No. 1 air-gun slugs. Air-guns and air-rifles are made in three sizes—Nos. 1, 2, and 3, of which No. 3 is the largest. The great majority are of No. 1 size, the calibre of which is ·177, or about one-sixth of an inch. But whatever the particular form of slug may be, the loss of force and likewise of accuracy occasioned by its not fitting the barrel with absolute perfection is as nothing compared to what is wasted at the breech so long as the hinged barrel is employed as the cocking-lever. Ordinary rifles and shotguns of however expensive a quality never depend for gas-tightness upon the close mechanical fit of the breech. The cartridge case acts in the well-known manner of the U-shaped washer in an air-pump, so that the greater the pressure the more tightly does the plastic case close all crevices. In the Millita as well as in the Gem type of air-gun the sole thing relied upon to prevent the escape of air was a leather washer at the cylinder orifice that was pressed outwards by the air against the breech-face to minimise the escape; but there was an escape all the same. This increased as the washer grew old, and things became doubly bad when the hinge got worn: and still greater irregularity of shooting followed.

The hinge itself is the main defect. Not only does it waste the air pressure obtained from the spring, but it very seriously affects the sighting. When the hinge gets loose the barrel wobbles, and then where are you? You can fairly wag the fore-sight about with your left hand, and you can see it jump with the shock of every discharge. Under such conditions shooting becomes simply ridiculous. Luck, indeed, may sometimes help you to a good diagram with a worn gun, but uniformity is the only true test. If you go on long enough you may get a single case of almost perfect pattern with almost any weapon. I once saw seven consecutive shots placed in a bull one-third of an inch in diameter at seven yards with an unrifled T-bar air-gun, which had been in use over ten years, shooting the common flanged slugs, but it was only a fluke. The gun never did it before or after. Yet by taking that as a " selected " pattern a man might have asserted with truth that the gun was " capable " of producing such a result. Granted. Yet it was a fluke all the same.

But there were ingenious minds at work to remedy the deficiencies of the air-gun. English people had begun to take a deeper interest in shooting, for the terrible lessons of the Boer War had not been quite wasted. An air-gun that could be depended upon to shoot as accurately as a cartridge weapon at a short range was absolutely needed. So we find that in 1904 patents were granted to Mr. Lincoln Jeffries for an air-rifle in which the barrel was made in one solid piece with the stock. The spring was compressed by means of a separate lever which was placed beneath the barrel, being hinged in front of the action. This obviated the necessity for the barrel being loose in order that it might be utilised as a lever, and such a thing as a barrel wobbling about like a broken toothpick at

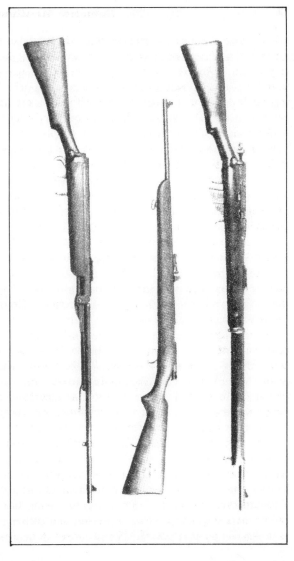

PLATE VIII

The Military Service Rifle.
The War Office Miniature Rifle.
The Military Pattern of the B.S.A. Air-Rifle.

once became a thing of the past. The barrel having been
made rigid, the problem next was how to introduce the
slug into it. Any return to the old muzzle-loading system
would have been ridiculous at the present day, so an
ingenious device was adopted. A steel plug which could
be rotated by an external handle was passed through the
barrel transversely at the breech and perforated with a
hole of the same calibre as the barrel at the point where
it came between the barrel and the orifice of the cylinder.
In fact, this was the principle of the breech-block of the
original pump air-gun, but it is really quite familiar to
all of us in the form of the ordinary tap by which the gas
in our houses is turned on and off. Such a tap is gas-tight
if the fit is perfect, which, after all, is only a matter of
mechanical accuracy; the theory of it is unimpeachable.

The introduction of the rotating breech-plug had
another object, however, in the modern air-rifle; it solved
the difficult problem of how to load. The handle was
rotated through an angle of 90 deg. so that the hole in it
was vertical and the orifice of the cylinder blocked. A
conical aperture was bored in the top of the action exactly
above the hole. A slug was dropped down this, and the
handle was rotated back again, thus unblocking the orifice
of the cylinder and bringing the slug into its proper
position at the bottom of the barrel; all that remained was
to press the trigger.

In 1905 the sole rights of manufacture under the
Jeffries patent were acquired by the Birmingham Small
Arms Company, and other patents have been taken out
to cover various improvements which have since been introduced into the arm. An air-rifle has now been put
on the market which possesses a perfectly rigid barrel and
a breech action that may be described as absolutely air-

tight. The result is that with a 10-grain slug a constant and uniform muzzle velocity of 500 feet per second can be attained, and an accuracy of flight ensured that enables diagrams to be made at 20 yards nearly on a par with those of an average ·22 rifle with rim-fire cartridges, and if anything superior to those of a Morris tube in a Service rifle. Beyond twenty yards the greater power of the powder cartridge with its higher velocity and heavier bullet is bound to assert itself; nevertheless, even at 50 and 100 yards some of the B.S.A. air-rifles have shown extraordinary excellence. For those of a mechanical turn of mind the sectional illustration pasted into the back cover of this volume will prove of great interest. It gives a knowledge of the internal mechanism which a casual outside glance cannot supply. I shot with one of these weapons at Bisley in 1905 and 1906, since when, to quote a certain famous gentleman of the road, I have used no other. For me it is the air-gun of the future.

CHAPTER V.

At Point-blank Range.

" POINT-BLANK " is a title, vainly invented, for a thing that does not exist—namely, a range at which a bullet goes absolutely straight to its destination. If one could find a part of space where gravitation does not act, one might find a point-blank range there. Till then we have to make the best of things as we know them on this planet, where the very instant the moving bullet loses the support of the barrel by leaving the muzzle, gravitation begins to draw it down towards the earth. From this conflict of forces the path of a bullet, fired from any sort of rifle, is bound to be a curve, the exact form of which depends mainly on the original velocity of the bullet, its weight and shape, and the resistance of the air. Full information as to these factors can be obtained in any of the standard works on gunnery. Meantime let us be content to assume that we can treat as point-blank any range at which our weapon will hit the bull with the sights normally adjusted. In the case of most air-guns we shall find this to be from five to ten yards, but with air-rifles having strong springs the distance is increased to twenty yards.

First, however, let us consider what we are going to

shoot at. We need a target, and we need a butt to stop the bullets. The gunsmiths, the co-operative stores, and the dealers in shooting accessories will generally supply these. Of butts, or bullet-stoppers, there are various forms. A very neat and popular one is made of steel, with a place in front for a card target to slip in and a sort of funnel behind to catch the bullets. Here let me say that this last is most important. Every bullet fired should be caught somehow. If you simply tack up a target against a tree and go shooting at it, chance decides what becomes of the bullets. Some may bury themselves in the bark or in the wood; others may fly off at an unknown angle. One of these may lodge in a human eye, and, small as the chance may be, it is a risk you have no right to take. Finally, the bullet may rebound towards the shooter, and the eye that is put out may be your own. Remember that a bullet may, and generally does, rebound from wood, or stone, or brick, or metal, indeed from almost anything.

My own method of catching the bullets has the merit of being cheap and simple. I get from the grocer an empty box of any ordinary size so long as it is not less than fifteen inches square and three inches deep. I nail two narrow strips of wood over the open top which is to be the front, fill the box with wood shavings or old papers, and place over them a stout piece of cardboard which retains the filling by being pushed under the two strips; lastly, I screw a handle on the top to carry it by, and the affair is complete. You may see what the combined target frame and stop-butt looks like in the Plate XII. The slugs perforate the cardboard front, and are absorbed by the filling, which keeps them from rebounding. Of course, if you miss the open front and hit the wooden strips you are liable to a rebound. Therefore, at first it is well to have the open front of a good size, say eighteen inches square; you can use a smaller one later.

The actual target, or bull's-eye with rings round it, can be bought cheap enough, as you will see by the dealers' price-lists. Sixpence to one shilling a hundred are common figures. However, I make my own on ordinary foolscap paper, and I use rubber stamps and an aniline inkpad. The stamps were made for me by Mr. Savage, of 96, Old Street, London, E.C., for about 3s. 6d. each. I recommend you to get two—one with the bull a quarter of an inch, inner ring half an inch, and magpie ring one inch in diameter, the other double this size. The smaller will do for a six yards range, the larger for twelve. For use at the longer ranges I generally buy targets of the N.R.A. or National Rifle Association standard sizes, which vary from time to time, but are now as follows :—

ORDINARY MINIATURE RIFLE TARGETS.

Divisions.	DIMENSIONS OF TARGETS.			
	4th Class, 100yds.	5th Class, 50yds.	6th Class, 25yds.	7th Class, 20yds.
Central... ...	2 in. dia.	none.	none.	none.
Bull	3½ ,, ,,	1¾in. dia.	$\frac{7}{8}$in. dia.	$\frac{7}{10}$in. dia.
Inner	6 ,, ,,	3 ,, ,,	1½ ,, ,,	1$\frac{2}{10}$,, ,,
Magpie... ...	9 ,, ,,	4½ ,, ,,	2¼ ,, ,,	1$\frac{8}{10}$,, ,,
Outer	Remainder of target. 24in. sq.	Remainder of target. 12in. sq.	Remainder of target. 6in. sq.	Remainder of target. 4$\frac{8}{10}$in. sq.

To affix the target to the cardboard front of the box I use paste, which keeps it from flapping in the wind out of doors, but clips or pins will serve. Now let us set the target at six yards off, or at twelve if we can get so long a distance, choosing a spot where there is a good wall or other obstacle to stop any bullet that might conceivably miss the box as well as target. Choose as level a place as you can in a good light, and spread down a rug or a piece of carpet to lie upon—a strip of old stair carpet measuring about two feet by six is excellent. If the ground seems damp put under it a waterproof or a strip of common strong green canvas that you can buy for two shillings a yard. Do not choose a place where you will lie in a hollow, nor one that is sloping in the least forward. The most suitable is one that, if anything, rises slightly towards the target. Lie down here and get yourself into a comfortable position ; shooting is a difficult art, and you will find it worth while to give yourself every chance. Do not let the box be in a line straight in front of the rug, but turn the foot of the rug a good yard to the left, so that when you lie down your body and legs will slant away leftwards. Take care not to crush your watch. Rest your elbows on the ground, the left hand grasping the rifle a little in front of the trigger-guard, while the right holds it by the grip, the thumb above, the first finger ready for the trigger. Some shooters pull the trigger with the second finger, as you may see some fine shots do at Bisley, but most men use the first. Let the other fingers grasp underneath, and hold the rifle firmly, with the butt well in to your shoulder. Point the barrel in the general direction of the target, take a look down the sights, and gradually work it round till they show just under the bull.

Do not squint too long down the sights at first. It is a strain on the eyes, and you do not want to begin by tiring them. Raise your head from the rifle and draw a few deep breaths. In order to breathe freely the lower part of the body only should press on the ground, and the chest should be sufficiently raised to give room to the lungs. For comfort, I prefer to lie with the legs moderately apart and perhaps one heel a little raised. But you must choose for yourself.

Now, having rested your eyes, look once more down the sights. Keep both eyes open, and, aiming with the right eye, bring the fore-sight into the V, as in the illustration : observe now what your left eye sees ; you will find that it sees the two sights indepen- dently. They are seen a bit to the 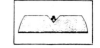 right of the view presented by the vision of the right eye, and they are not in line, but one a little behind the other. If you are to become a two-eyed shot you must be able to disregard these left-eye sights in aiming and concentrate on the right-eye sights, using the left eye only to look at the bull. If, as will probably be the case, you decide that for the pre- sent you will not go in for learning two-eyed shoot- ing, you must close the left eye again and aim afresh at the bull. Take care that the fingers do not block the line of sight on top of the barrel. If you cannot close the left eye without the right half-closing also, you will find a patch over the left eye, consisting of a bit of brown paper tied round your head, an easy remedy.

Now once more look down the sights at the bull. Let the bull balance itself, as it were, on top of them, taking the fore-sight full. A full sight is the easiest to catch, and, therefore, most men use it in quick work, such as game- shooting. A fine sight, given perfect eyes and nerves, renders possible a more accurate and uniform alignment of the barrel, and it is, therefore, largely used by target shots, even by men who would always take a full sight at game. But the fine sight is a counsel of perfection; the Government rule for young soldiers is that they should learn to take a full sight, and the ordinary beginner had better take his sight full. So let the top of the fore-sight come level with the top of the notch and almost touch the bull at 6 o'clock. Position on the target 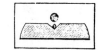 is indicated by imagining it to be marked like the dial of a clock.

Now, for a change, close both eyes for a minute to rest them, and pay attention to your hands. You can feel that your left hand is supporting most of the weight of the rifle, as it is bound to do, for it holds the rifle near the centre of gravity in front of the trigger-guard. Standing up it is possible to extend the left arm nearly straight and hold the rifle close to the muzzle, though few men do so. But, lying down, you must bend your elbow and hold further back. The exact grip in holding varies. Some men grip tight with the left, and pull the rifle strongly in to the shoulder; others grip more lightly—in fact, they hardly do more than allow the rifle to rest on the palm. Experience will show which suits you best. But it is a thing that you must pay attention to, because the vibrations of the barrel set up by the discharge of a shot (and this is equally true of an air-gun and of a .303 Lee-Enfield) are affected by the grip of the left hand, and these vibrations affect the shot. If your grip is uniform you may expect, other things being

PLATE IX

Whether for adjusting the sight or instructing the beginner, rest shooting has many advantages if used in reason

equal, a uniform result on the target, but if you alternately grip loose and tight you will find the shots vary. This is an important thing to remember.

Next observe your grip with the right hand, whether it is tight or the reverse. This also affects the shot. I myself believe strongly in a firm grip with the right.

Open the right eye and take a full sight on the bull. Put the forefinger round the trigger—well round, so that the junction of the first and second joints presses it—and squeeze downwards with the thumb. As the rifle is not yet cocked nothing happens, only you will feel the trigger yield under the squeeze. This is the right way of giving the release. We talk of pulling the trigger, but the trigger should not be pulled but squeezed off. Try the effect of giving it a sharp pull instead of a steady backward pressure. Do you not feel at once that the tendency is to pull round the muzzle of the rifle sideways to the right? One of the commonest causes of shooting to the right is this pull of the forefinger.

The pull-off of a trigger may vary from one pound up to ten; it is measured by the cocked rifle being held vertically, when the weight that the trigger will lift before it goes off is the amount of the pull. One of ten pounds is very heavy; one of a pound or less is known as a hairtrigger. The Lee-Enfield long rifle has a five pounds pull-off, which is a trifle heavy, but answers well enough. The Lee-Enfield trigger is stiff, and does not yield to pressure till the last moment. Others " creep " when pressed till they go off suddenly at the end; this is known as the " drag " pull, and it has been adopted for the new Service rifle. Good shooting can be done with either.

Let your cheek rest, not so much on the top of the stock as against the side of it, and mind you do not cant

the head over to the right more than you can help ; hold
your head as upright and as far back as you can.   This
will keep your face from getting bruised by the kick when
you come to fire the ·303, and it will also give your eye
a better focus.   Every inch further back that your eye is
from the back-sight the clearer you can see it.

All this preliminary exercise may seem tedious to
anyone who is anxious to begin plugging away at the
target at once, but it is best to go through with it.   If
you get down—" get down " is the technical phrase the
range officer uses when he tells you that it is your turn
to do your shoot—if you get down anyhow, and start with
wrong habits, you may find it hard to shake them off
afterwards.   I know it seems tedious not to loose off as
soon as you have a rifle in your fist.   You naturally want
to hear the shot go up against the target with a thud
and then to see where it hits.   Nevertheless the very best
shots in England find it worth their while to practise
aiming without firing.   I have been told that Sergeant-
Major Wallingford, of the Hythe School of Musketry,
will spend an hour a day practising for a big shoot in
simply snapping an empty rifle.   But he does not snap
it at random ; each shot is aimed as carefully as on the
range, and after the trigger has been pressed and the
cocking-piece has snapped he " holds on "—that is to
say, he keeps the sights still bearing on the bull, noting
the slightest aberration.   Though there has been no discharge, he can tell what his shot would have done by
thinking about it.

Thinking about it—that is the essence of perfect
shooting.   What the caddie boy proudly said of golf is
also true of the rifle, " This game is played with the
head."

CHAPTER VI.

The Baptism of Fire.

A BAPTISM of fire is what I hope you will be able to give the target after all these preliminaries. You must take your air-gun, if it is one of the older type, and release the catch, bend the barrel down, compress the spring, and insert the slug into the breech, as shown in Plate XI. Remember the rat-trap.

Holding it in this position, you may if you like put a drop of oil into the orifice of the cylinder, in order to oil the piston. I never put in much for fear of softening unduly the leather pad or cushion which protects the piston-head, but a little occasionally is useful. Some of the oil will be driven down the barrel by the first discharge, and the next shot with an oily barrel is pretty sure to go wild. It is the same with the Service rifle, and an oily barrel is the true explanation of some unaccountable misses at Bisley. The humble air-gun will teach one this lesson; and with it there can be no doubt as to the true explanation, for in the case of the air-gun slug you will find an oily mark where it has gone into the target.

It tends to regularity of shooting if you push the slug a quarter or half an inch into the barrel. A seater like a stout bradawl cut down to half an inch long will do this in a uniform way. This prevents the slug from sticking at the entrance to the chamber. Slugs, especially the cheaper ones, are apt to vary slightly in diameter, and therefore do not all enter with equal ease. The seater ensures them all the same start.

Now close the action by taking the butt in the right hand and raising it while the left hand holds the barrel slanting forwards and downwards. If the gun goes off accidentally (and you never can tell) the bullet will then only strike the ground, whereas if you close the action by raising the barrel to a horizontal position everything within range is in danger from the discharge. With a B.S.A. air-rifle the *modus operandi* is as follows : Hold it firmly in the right hand, nearly upright, with the butt pressed securely against the hollow of your thigh, and grasp the lever with the left hand, as shown in the Plate opposite. Now press the thumb strongly against the barrel, and the lever will detach itself. The lever should next be depressed till the click is heard, which signifies that the trigger has caught the piston, after which it must be raised again to its original position.

Now hold the rifle with the muzzle pointing a little downwards in the direction of the target, so that it cannot point at your neighbour. If you acquire the habit of always loading with the muzzle towards the target you will save many a nerve shock to your friends. Also the regulations order you to do so on every rifle range.

Turn up the handle of the rotating breech-plug as far as it will go, so that the hole of it corresponds exactly to the conical recess above. Drop a slug into the hole, and if it does not drop down freely of itself push it into place with a match or other pointed implement. Turn

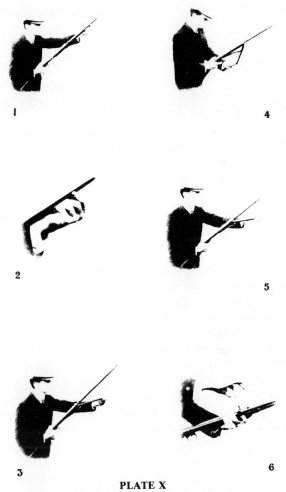

PLATE X

Loading positions for the B.S.A. Air-Rifle. Showing the
method of opening the cocking lever, the position of the hand
when releasing the retaining catch, and so forth till the slug
is inserted preparatory to firing

down the handle till it checks, and the arm is now loaded, cocked, and ready for action.

Some men load lying down, and so have only to turn over in order to get into position for shooting, but I myself prefer to rise, and I always load standing up or kneeling. Whatever position you adopt you must now lie down, get comfortable, aim at the bull, and press the trigger. You will find it difficult to keep distinctly before your mind all the different maxims we have laid down. There are at least a dozen of them :

Head back.
Head up.
Head steady.
Eye well open.
Eye on the bull.
Hand-grip firm, but not too hard.
First finger-joint on trigger.
Press thumb down.
Breathe out slowly.
Hold the breath.
Squeeze off release.

That will be enough for awhile, though there are more if you can think them out. It may be a comfort to you to know that when a golfer takes his stance on the tee and addresses his ball for the drive there are fifteen different things he ought to think of at once. The strain seems almost too much for the human mind. Did not the centipede's brain give way when he was asked which of his hundred legs went after which? And the centipede's brain (if he has one) got an earlier start in the evolutionary race than ours.

Now that you have fired your shot, try to spot your bullet mark. One great advantage of air-gunning is that

you are your own marker. At 100 yards or over you re-
quire a man at the butts to signal the value of your shot,
and to show you just where it struck by putting a
spotting-disc on the target. But at six yards, and even at
twelve yards, you can spot for yourself with the unassisted
eye if your eyesight is good; you certainly can if you take
even a small opera-glass or field-glass to aid you. With
a really good field-glass or a moderate telescope you may
spot very well up to fifty yards. Of course the shots on
the white are easily distinguished, but beyond fifty yards
one needs a first-class three-inch refracting telescope to
separate the shots on the bull. If you use a telescope,
fix it on a good stand, and you will find that it tires your
eye much less. When I am using a telescope I prefer
to arrange it handy for the left eye. Then the right,
which has to take the strain of aiming, gets a rest while
the left is busy spotting.

Look then at your target, and if you see your shot on
the bull it is probable that you aimed straight and the
sights were right. In that case, go on and prosper. But
if your shot is off the bull you have to discover the cause
and remedy it. Reload and fire again with the same aim.
Don't change it. If the shot strikes near the first it is
probable that the sights are wrong. But, to make certain,
fire a few more shots, always with the same aim. If they
are all close together you may take it for certain that the
sights want altering.

If your sights are not adjustable, your best remedy is
to alter them temporarily with gum and black paper. If
you want to make the shots go higher, gum a strip along
the top of the back-sight; experiment alone will tell you
how much is required. A general rule will give some
guidance, viz. : For ten yards range, an inch correction

of the shooting is made by the 20th of an inch correction
on the sights; for twenty yards, the same alteration makes
two inches difference to the shooting. Cut a notch in the
paper exactly over the old one if the shots were straight
but low; cut it to the left if they struck to the right and
vice versâ.

Put on a fresh target; never be stingy of targets.
It is annoying to waste time in trying to spot your shots
after the target has had its baptism of fire. Targets are
cheap. With a stamp I think I can make a hundred in
five minutes, and even if you manufacture them with a
paint-brush and ink you will probably turn out a dozen
in less than a quarter of an hour. So treat yourself to a
fresh target, and try your new arrangement of the sights
on that. By shifting the notch from side to side, or a
little lower or higher, you can soon get it so that the
bullets group on or round the bull, and then your problem
is solved.

But supposing that they go very high, you cannot
bring them down, because you cannot bring the paper
addition to the back-sight lower than the original top of
the sight. You must, therefore, raise the fore-sight by
sticking paper on it till the desired effect has been produced, and by the time you have got through you will
have learned a good deal about sighting a rifle. Of course
a gunsmith can put you on proper steel sights of the right
height, and if one of the sights is mounted in a dovetail-
notch, delicate manipulation with a hammer and brass
punch or copper coin will enable you to make lateral cor-
rections.

If, however, your air-rifle is fitted with an elevating
back-sight the business is simpler. The B.S.A. rifle
shown in Plate VIII. and others has a Lee-Enfield ·303

military back-sight specially fitted to it. The rifle which the cadet boys are using for garden practice is built to reproduce the weight, length, and shape of the ·303 long Lee-Enfield. With this sight you slip the slide forwards up the leaf, which causes the leaf to rise on the ramp, and gives you any elevation desired. The ordinary pattern of B.S.A. rifle has not got this sight, but one in which the change of elevation is obtained by turning a milled disc under the sight. The net result is the same. You can make the shots strike higher or lower at pleasure.

In order to make them strike to the right or left I use the sliding wind-gauge on the back-sight, which has now been sanctioned by the N.R.A. There are various forms of this, but they all provide a slide which can be adjusted laterally by pushing it or by turning a milled screw.

We will assume, then, that your air-gun or air-rifle has been adjusted, either by yourself or by a gunsmith, so that the sights are true. We will now consider what sort of a diagram you can get with it on the target. If the shots do not all strike on or close to the $\frac{1}{4}$in. bull at six yards or the $\frac{1}{2}$in. at twelve yards there is something wrong, and the source of the wrong may be in you or in the weapon. Which of the two is to blame is hard for you to decide, but an expert friend will enlighten you in five minutes. He has only to fire a dozen carefully-aimed shots into the target and he will know exactly what the gun is doing. A high-class air-rifle should be capable of placing all the shots on the bull. An air-gun or rifle which is partially worn or was originally of poorer quality may be able to place most of its shots within the inner ring, with an occasional wild one outside. The common smooth-bored air-gun cannot be depended on to

PLATE XI

View showing the special method of holding hinged-barrel Air-
Guns to prevent injury to the fingers should the spring escape
from the retaining catch on the trigger

do better than score magpies, with a considerable percentage of outers. No good shot would care to shoot much with any other than the first quality. The moment he finds that he sometimes makes bulls and sometimes magpies when he knows he was holding true on the bull he loses his interest. It has become a game of chance for him. Yet the beginner may be able to find both profit and pleasure with a weapon that the expert would despise. The beginner's shots may wander all over a six-inch circle; an air-gun whose margin of error is about an inch will do him well enough till he has reduced his own six-inch margin to two.

So plug away at your target, and do your best to give it its baptism of fire. Do not fire too fast, and yet it is well not to linger too long on the aim. When you have got used to it you will find that you can loose off within three seconds of the moment when you fairly get the sights to bear. Sometimes you can loose off in the first second, sometimes you must wait. In snap-shooting you will find that you positively must let fly in that first second, but one must learn to walk before one can run, and I doubt the wisdom of trying to begin as a snap-shooter. Nevertheless my advice is not to dwell on the aim longer than you can help.

But though I would not have you dwell, I would have you "hold on." The habit of seeing the sights under the bull after the shot has been discharged is excellent. By this you may judge whether you flinched, or wobbled off, or pulled the muzzle round with the trigger forefinger, or depressed it at the moment of firing. Try to learn a lesson from every shot. If it failed to hit where you intended there was a reason for it. Think it out. This is one of the great uses of shooting. It worries you. Hand and eye alone are not enough. You must use your brain. I have heard among schoolboys the cheap sneer, " Oh, any fool can shoot," but all it means is that the sneerer wishes to belittle some fellow who is no great hand at cricket, and yet shoots better than the captain of the eleven. Well, if the captain cannot shoot straight, more's the pity, but be assured that the boy who can put on a possible for his school in the Spencer Cup or the Ashburton Shield at Bisley is no fool with a rifle.

The Ashburton shield is the prize competed for by teams from the public schools; the Spencer Cup is for the best individual score made by members of the teams.

So plug away and try to reach a " possible " with the air-rifle. A " possible " is a highest possible score, which consists of an unbroken string of bulls; in a seven-shot shoot this would be : 5, 5, 5, 5, 5, 5, 5 — 35. Seven is the usual number of shots at one distance in ordinary competitions. It is chosen as high enough to exclude fluking. Anybody may, by a sheer fluke, make one bull, or perhaps two consecutively, or even, though very seldom, three. But it is a million to one against fluking seven bulls running. In the severer competitions at the more difficult distances, ten-shot and even twenty-shot shoots are not unusual. They are intended to give a due advantage to the man who, after finding what allowance on the target is necessary to hit the bull, succeeds best in keeping on it. But that introduces the question of allowance for wind and weather, which we must leave for another chapter.

So try for a seven-shot possible of 35 with your air-rifle with all the intelligence at your command, and one of the things you will soon discover is that a very con-

siderable advantage can be gained by using the sling.
You will see how it is used by the boys in uniform. Military rifles are provided with a sling, which is primarily intended for carrying the weapon slung over one shoulder, thus leaving the rifleman's hands free. But it is also employed to steady the rifle in aiming, for which purpose it is fastened to two swivels, one near the muzzle and one just in front of the trigger guard. It should hang about four feet long, the precise length being settled by the length of the rifle barrel and the size of the rifleman's arm. In order to shoot with it on, the left arm is put through the sling up to the shoulder; then the left hand is lowered and brought out leftwards under the sling, and then up and over it till the hand grasps the rifle near the back-sight. The sling should neither be too tight nor too slack (I prefer it just a little slack), but the loop should have a distinct pull against the upper arm, which is well seen in several of the Plates.

In shooting standing up the gain given by the sling is considerable, but the advantage is most fully felt in the prone position. After keeping some scores made with the sling and without, I have come to the conclusion that for me its average value is two points in a possible 35. Doubtless men vary in this, and I know one fine shot who never uses it at all, but most men prefer to avail themselves of all the help they can get from it.

A military sling for carrying purposes is $1\frac{1}{4}$ inch wide, but merely as an aid to shooting it is enough if it be only an inch or even no wider than an ordinary strap. The B.S.A. air-rifle can be had with eyes or rings, to which the sling may be attached by spring-hooks. I fit rings for the same purpose to my old-fashioned air-guns by means of leather loops, which are made fast to the barrel by inserting them between it and a wooden forehand affixed to the barrel by a binding of strong waxed twine. I find that the boys who shoot with my air-guns highly appreciate the sling, and learn to use it with good effect.

Shooting is not a solitary sport. One can practise by oneself if necessary, but it is far more enjoyable when two or three friends get down side by side, and compare notes, and exhibit a little friendly rivalry over scores. It is by watching those who are better performers than oneself that one can improve one's style most rapidly, and one learns also by teaching. When I have a squad of boys at work I find it pays well to set the more advanced to coach the tyros ; they all profit thereby. The pride, the very proper pride, of the teacher acts on himself as a stimulus. *Docendo disces.*

CHAPTER VII.

Long-range Shooting and Wind Allowance.

HITHERTO we have been working at point-blank range; that is to say, the line joining the fore- and back-sights has pointed straight at the target, and so also, practically speaking, has the axis of the rifle barrel. But when we come to long-range work, at 500, or 1000, or 1100 yards, the axis of the barrel must no longer point straight at the target, because, as was pointed out in Chapter V., owing to the action of gravity the bullet begins to drop as soon as it leaves the muzzle. In order to reach the distant mark, therefore, the muzzle of the barrel must be tilted up to the proper angle, so that the bullet may first rise and then drop just enough to attain the point desired. The curved path described by the bullet through the air is called its trajectory; this curve varies in different rifles, and with modern small-bores it is much flatter than in the older makes. At 500 yards the path of the .303 bullet, at its highest point, rises only 4 feet above the direct line of sight, at 1000 yards it rises 25 feet, and at 2000 yards, 190 feet. To make the muzzle point sufficiently upwards that the bullet may rise to these heights,

the ·303 Lee-Enfield rifle, like every other military
weapon, is provided with an elevating back-sight; this
when erect stands up about $2\frac{1}{4}$ inches, and it carries a bar
that slides up and down and has the regulation V notch
in the middle; on the elevating leaf of the back-sight are
drawn lines at distances varying from $\frac{1}{8}$ to $\frac{1}{4}$ of an inch,
and marked 6, 7, 8, 9, 10, etc. These figures mean so
many hundreds of yards. By sliding the bar up, say to
the 8, you know that the .303 rifle when fired with service
ammunition at a target 800 yards away ought to throw
the bullet dead on the mark.

Now, though the air-rifle is only adapted for short
ranges under 50 yards, it is quite possible to practise
with it in a way that will make you perfectly familiar with
the rifleman's methods of work at 800 yards. For this
purpose you must procure an air-rifle fitted at the manu-
factory with a Lee-Enfield back-sight, or else you must get
a gunsmith to put one on for you, and you had better have
him also provide a sight protector for it, which will probably cost you from ten to fifteen shillings altogether. I
like to have the military sight put on at the same distance
down the barrel in front of the trigger as the sight of the
Lee-Enfield, so that the eye grows accustomed to the ser-
vice-rifle conditions, and I also prefer to have the bed
adjusted to the barrel at such an angle that when the leaf
is elevated and the bar slid down to the very bottom, the
rifle shoots true for short-range work.

Now to put the method in practice. Take your rubber
stamp and stamp it twice on a piece of paper, so that
one bull's-eye is, say, 4 inches from the other. Paste
this up so that the line joining the two bull's-eyes is
vertical, and set the sliding bar on the upright leaf at 8.
You can do this with the finger and thumb of one hand

or with your two thumbs, one on each side ; but remember
what Izaak Walton recommends the angler to do when
putting a live frog on his hook : " Handle him tenderly,
as if you loved him." Treat your sight like the frog, and
do not strain or bend the leaf in any way ; teach yourself
to adjust it with the minute dexterity of a watchmaker,
and you will find it of real service to you on the range.
Most riflemen, however, do not trust their thumbs, but
perform the operation by means of a vernier. This is a
neat little instrument, sold by all the opticians who deal
in riflemen's equipment at from five to ten shillings. If
you buy one you should, if possible, make the seller show
you how to use it, or in any case make him give you full
printed directions. The vernier is made to fit on the ·303
leaf, and by turning a screw you can raise the bar the
150th of an inch at a time. Shooting men usually describe these 150ths as so many degrees. The more fas-
tidious call them " points," because the actual angle
represented is one minute, of which there are sixty in a
degree. You may hear a rifleman going to the 800 yards,
after the 600, say to his friend, " Well, I had 26deg.
on at the six and that seemed all right. I think I shall
put on nineteen more for the eight." And you will see
him sit down with his rifle across his lap, and take the
vernier out of his pouch or his pocket and delicately screw
up his sliding bar from the reading of 26deg. to 45deg. on
his scale. But the rough-and-ready man who uses his
thumbs to move it from line 6 to line 8 on the leaf often
makes just as good a score. The vernier is not indispensable.

So let us suppose that we begin with our thumbs. Lie
down with the leaf upright and the bar at 800 yards, and
shoot at the lower bull's-eye. The slug ought to hit the

paper somewhere up in the neighbourhood of the upper target. Just where it hits will depend upon the exact number of yards between the rifle and the target, and also upon the exact distance between the upright leaf and the fore-sight. Also it will depend upon whether you held the rifle truly vertical or not. If you did, the slug should hit the paper somewhere in a vertical line above the lower bull; if, however, you canted the rifle over so that the leaf leaned to the right, you may expect to find the bullet hole to the right of the line. It is all-important to keep the leaf upright. Match rifles are generally fitted with a little spirit-level to show when the sight is truly perpendicular, but this is too elaborate for the service arm and is not permitted in ordinary competitions. For the present you may disregard the question of actually hitting the upper bull's-eye, and go on shooting till you are clear that you can hold the rifle upright and keep the slugs well on the vertical line.

Now, if they are striking straight, but are considerably below the upper target, you must raise the bar above the line marked 8 on the leaf. Move it a little at a time. An inch is a great deal in a man's nose, and the 150th of an inch counts for something on the sight of a ·303. Some men can manipulate their sights to 3-150ths of an inch with nothing but their fingers. See if you can rival them. Feel your way thus up to the bull, altering your elevation after each shot. Of course, if the slugs went too high at first you must lower the bar instead. But proceed by lowering, or raising, or both, till you have got the exact elevation at which a shot aimed at the lower bull will strike in the upper one. Continue to practise at this, and you will be interested to see how precisely each shot on the upper target answers to your aim on the

PLATE XII

Portable Target Apparatus for Air-Rifle Shooting

NOTE—As air-gun bullets are apt to rebound if they strike wood, the gap behind the targets should be at least six inches in height, or even more for a beginner

lower. If you aim at three o'clock you get a three—three
o'clock describes the location of the shot on the target,
which is to be considered as a clock-face—if you aim
at nine you get a nine, and so on.   Now you begin
to see how a man has to adjust his sights for long-
range work with the ·303. He has more than the mere
number of yards to consider.   The normal elevation for
800 yards with the ·303 is 45deg., but the condition of
the light may cause this to vary one or two or even three
degrees, more or less.   Bright sunshine, rain, a cloudy sky,
the force of the wind, and the approach of sunset, all
affect the exact elevation to be given to the sights.   When
a man starts to shoot at a particular range he must use
his judgment as to what to allow ; then, if he is both lucky
and skilful he may find the bull the first time with his
sighting shot—or sighter, as it is called—after which, if
he is shooting well, he will keep on the bull or near it.
But if he is not lucky, if the wind deceives him, if the air
and the light are adverse—in short, if for any reason he
has not gauged the conditions with sufficient accuracy—he
is liable to begin with a miss, after which he will surely
be compelled to feel his way shot by shot first to the target
and then to the bull's-eye, just as described above.

You may, of course, repeat this experiment at the
ranges indicated by the other figures 6 or 7 or 9, etc.   I
chose the 800 because that is one of the most common
distances in competitions, and it is therefore well to
accustom yourself to the look of the sights at that elevation and to the feel of the gun.   With the 800 sight up
your head has to be held distinctly higher, with the result
that you get a slightly different pressure of the cheek
against the butt and of the butt against the shoulder,
which makes a change in the way of holding to which you

must learn to adjust yourself. The old hand does all these things instinctively.

Perhaps the best piece of shooting at the 800 yards I ever saw was at Lydd, where there were a number of competitions being carried on simultaneously. Corporal V., who was among the best shots in the Army, had been shooting in a competition at the 1000 yards. The moment it was over he hurried to the 800, where there was another one going on in which he was also entered. But as he got to the long bank where the 800 yards competitors had been shooting he saw the men streaming away and the scorers taking down the blackboards on which they keep the scores and picking up their chairs. Competitions have to be concluded by a definite time, and the time was just up. V. ran to the range officer and asked to be allowed to take his turn. " Too late," said the officer. " You can't begin now. You would have to fire ten shots, and it's only three minutes to the hour for closing."

" Give me a chance, sir," cried V., flinging himself down on the banquette. " Give me three targets." It takes about a minute on the average for each target to be lowered and examined for score and raised again. With only one target he would have required ten minutes or more.

" All right," said the officer, " you can have targets 7, 8, 9."

The scorers dropped back into their chairs; the nearest one handed to V. his eleven cartridges—ten shots to count and one sighter.

V. shoved his bar to the 8 with his thumbs; no time for verniers. Bang he went, bull! Bang, again, and a bull was signalled on the next target! Bang, and a bull on the third! He got his eleven shots in before the time

was up, and his score was 46 out of a possible 50.   I
wish we had three hundred thousand men like him in the
British Army.

Of course V. could not have done this unless he had
known the wind, but he had got that from his shoot at
the 1000 yards.   At long ranges the allowance to be made
for wind is all-important.   If you go to the 600 yards
range with a ·303 on a day when there is a fresh wind
blowing across the range, say from left to right, a bullet
aimed straight at the bull's-eye will be blown clean off
the target and strike in the stop butt some two feet outside the right-hand edge of the target altogether.   A
rifleman would describe such a wind as a five-foot wind
from the left, or at nine o'clock.   In describing the wind
you call it twelve o'clock if it blows in your face, or
six o'clock if it is at your back, and so on.   To compensate for the deflection thus caused he must make his rifle-
barrel point five feet to the left of the bull.   But when he
tries to do this by pointing his sights there he finds that
the white target and the black bull do not come behind
the V at all, but have disappeared behind the right-hand
part of the sliding bar, thereby leaving him only the dull
colour of the stop butt to define his fore-sight against.
Men have made excellent scores even under these adverse
circumstances, but only by the very best of eyesight and
judgment aided by a little luck.   If, however, a man can
alter his back-sight so as to make it move sideways to the
left, and then aim over it straight at the bull, he can
thus make the axis of the barrel point up-wind to the
left of the bull, while he has the advantage of the white
target as a background for his sights.   The exact amount
to which the back-sight must be moved to compensate for
a given strength of wind at a given range has been found

by experiment, and tables will be found in all the score-register books sold by the dealers in riflemen's equipment, which will give you full details.

Up to 1906 our riflemen were not allowed to use any form of back-sight on the ·303 rifle capable of lateral movement, though the soldiers of most foreign Powers already had one on their weapons. Now, however, an adjustable sight has been officially sanctioned, and any gunsmith can procure one for about 3s. 6d. and put it on the leaf of the ·303 sight of your air-rifle instead of the plain bar. Supposing that you have had this done, you should now paste two targets side by side on the front of your box with, say, an interval of 1½ inches between them, lie down, say, at ten yards range, push the slide a little to the left in the slot, aim at the right-hand target, and try a shot. Assuming that you have got the elevation correct, the slug should strike somewhere on a line joining the two bull's-eyes. Now shift the slide a little more or a little less to the left, just as you moved the bar up or down vertically in finding the elevation for 800 yards, and thus feel your way, until when you shoot at the right-hand bull you find you can hit the left. This is precisely what the rifleman does when he is troubled by a strong wind blowing across the range.

Supposing, however, that you have not procured a sliding sight, you may use the ordinary bar to obtain the same effect in the following way. Look at the cap which is dovetailed on the top of the leaf and you will see a small screw in it. Take out this (remember Izaak Walton's frog!), remove the cap, take off the bar and turn it upside down, so that the V is at the lower side, and replace the parts as before. You now have on the leaf a straight bar to look over instead of one with a V in the middle.

If you prefer it you can buy for 1s. 6d. a special match-bar to put on which has no V at all. Take your vernier, and find the exact middle of the bar, or else guess it by the eye as near as you can. Take your paint-box, which should contain a cake of good Chinese white as well as some dead black for blackening both the fore- and the back-sights. With a fine paint-brush draw a thin vertical white line on the bar in the middle. It is considered best not to draw the line right up to the top of the bar, but to leave a minute interval.

Paste up two targets about $1\frac{1}{2}$ inches apart, as you did before, and draw a second white line to the left of the middle of the bar. Probably 10deg. measured by the vernier will be somewhere about right. If you have no vernier try 1-12th or 1-16th of an inch. It is impossible to say precisely, because the distance between the fore-sight and the back-sight on your rifle and the length of your range will affect the amount. Lie down and aim at the right-hand bull over your left-hand line. As before, assuming your elevation to be correct, the slug should strike somewhere on a line joining the two. If it hits the left-hand bull you have, metaphorically speaking, got the wind just right. If not, you must alter your left line until an aim truly taken at the right-hand bull sends the slug on to the left. If the original divergence of the slug is large, you will find it better to draw a fresh line entirely, but if it is small, you may prefer to let the original line remain on the bar, and to take your aim over one edge of it instead of over the middle. Some men like to draw two lines, say at ten and twelve degrees, and try shots first over one, and then between them, and then over the other, till they are satisfied. Men with very good eyesight can make astonishingly fine divisions

of their white lines as they look at their fore-sight over
the top of the straight bar, and such men can make
infinitesimal allowances from one shot to the next according as they judge the wind to be changing in strength
and direction.

Judging the wind is one of the most puzzling and
exasperating of the problems that the rifleman has to
solve. On the range he sees provided on purpose to help
him a row of flags on tall poles, set generally one
hundred yards apart, along each side. He watches how
the flags blow, and guesses the force and direction of
the wind by that, and guides himself accordingly. You
cannot do this on a ten or twenty yards range, but you
can make a sort of imitation of it. Take your rubber
stamp and stamp a row of eight targets as near as you
can guess by eye 1½ inches apart, and paste this up in
a horizontal position.

Now, with the sights adjusted laterally as described
above, shoot at one that stands No. 2 from the left.
Presumably you will get a bull on No. 1. Now look at
No. 3 from the left. Is the distance between 3 and 2
the same as between 2 and 1 ; or is it less, or more? In
stamping the targets rapidly by hand you may very possibly have varied to some such extent as one-eighth of an
inch in the distance between them. That would about
correspond to a change of six inches in the wind's force
at 500 yards. Such a change is the commonest thing
possible in actual work on the range. Judge with your
eye what the variation is and allow accordingly in your
next shot, which, of course, must be aimed at the third
bull ; continue to do this all down the line and see what
your score is for the seven. Be resolute with yourself
not to go on blindly aiming at the next target without

using your brains; think it out before each shot just
how much or how little you want to alter your sighting,
if at all; the problem you set yourself to solve will be
exactly parallel to that which has to be tackled by the
rifleman at 500 or 800 yards on a windy day. A wind
is seldom quite steady; almost always there are alternate
puffs and lulls, and the shooter who bangs away, ignoring
these, will find his score most annoyingly irregular.
Corporal V. had this one advantage in having only three
minutes for his shoot. It left the wind less time to
change, so that he could concentrate his whole attention
on accuracy of aim. He didn't have to think of anything
except steady trigger-pulling the moment he got his aim.

Instead of having the ·303 Lee-Enfield sight fitted
to your air-rifle, you may of course have any other
elevating sight you prefer. The new Service rifle,
the ·303 Lee-Enfield, short, as it is technically
termed, has a back-sight which is a great improvement on that of the long rifle. And on the
cadet rifle which has been officially approved a modifica-
tion of the new sight suitable to the smaller arm has been
adopted. The elevating arrangement is different from the
old, and is so contrived that the slide itself carries its
own vernier, so to speak, both for the vertical and lateral
adjustments needful. It would be an excellent plan to
have one of these on your air-rifle and make yourself
familiar with its manipulation. Ultimately, when the
new rifle comes to be placed in the hands of volunteers
and civilians generally, the advantage of this will be
obvious, but while we have to do our cartridge shooting
with the Lee-Enfield long rifle, I prefer to stick to the
back-sight that belongs to it. There has been much con-
troversy about the respective merits of the long and short

Service rifles; both are good weapons, though they have certain deficiencies. But there are many men who think that the Lee-Enfield, long, if it were adapted for rapid loading with a charger, and fitted with the new sight, would be a good enough weapon for anybody.

PLATE XIII

Mr. Maurice Blood, the celebrated Rifle and Revolver Shot, testing the Military Pattern
B.S.A. Air-Rifle by the use of Magnifying Match Sights

CHAPTER VIII.

Snapshooting and the Running Man.

SHOOTING at a fixed target with unlimited time for taking your aim is the task set you in ordinary competitions; but snapshooting is also provided for, and it is a most valuable preparation for actual work in the field. You are given a certain number of cartridges to fire at a target, which generally is made to represent an enemy's head and shoulders. You are told either to get off as many shots as you can in so many seconds by the watch, or else, if the target be one that alternately appears and disappears, to fire every time you see it. Very great speed can be attained by a man using a rifle fitted with a magazine that can be quickly refilled by means of packets of cartridges held in a clip or charger. Loading an air-gun requires more time, and to get off from six to ten aimed shots in a minute is good work. Most men find that they can get their aim quickest by taking a full bead and sighting rather under the mark. The full bead is easier to catch, and compensates for the low sighting. To make an air-gun target of the disappearing class, I use one with a hinged flap-front, which can be pulled up and lowered again by the man holding the watch. Five seconds up and five down is a good allowance to begin with, but after you have got into practice you will be able to shorten the time considerably. To make a man a truly useful comrade in a tight place I do not know of any better form of practice than rapid shooting against time. This snapshooting at a fixed target leads up to shooting at a moving one in the case of any man who really intends to become a master of his weapon. In wild countries men learn to shoot running, through the necessity they are under of killing deer or other game for food. In Great Britain, where the coveted privilege of slaying a single stag is estimated to cost at least £50, such opportunities are scarcer. Nevertheless, as in some other things, civilisation is able to provide a fairly effective substitute. At Bisley there is a little railway track laid down, 55 yards long, which dips a yard and a half in the middle. Behind it rises a steep bank of sandy soil covered over with a thick growth of bushes. Beside the track and in front of it there is placed a low embankment just high enough to hide a little trolley car that runs along the track. At each end there is a big, strong butt for the markers, and into this the trolley runs. There are two stage dummies made of canvas, one representing rudely the life-size figure of a man, the other that of a deer. The men in the butt place the man or the deer on the trolley, and start him off with a good shove. The khaki-coloured dummy slips silently out from behind the big butt, but be careful : you are not allowed to shoot at him yet ; he runs for 5 yards, half seen, behind a thin screen of bushes till he reaches a white post, whence he rushes swiftly downhill to the bottom of the dip, and then his accumulated momentum carries him up the opposite slope. Here is placed another white post, which is his point of safety, and then he travels on, past a second screen of bushes, till he finally vanishes, as silently as he appeared, into the other markers'· butt. The markers examine his wound (if any), signal the result to the firing point, patch him up, turn him round, and start him on his perilous journey back again.

It really is a very amusing game to watch, as well as to play. The shooter stands intent, his rifle held, according to the rule, below his elbow; the mysterious figure glides forth into the open; the rifle comes up, comes level, goes off; there is a splash of yellow sand on the bank behind the runner, yet, though he be hit through the heart, the victim makes no sign; he offers no more resistance than a ghost, and he vanishes like one. And then we all watch eagerly for the tell-tale scoring disk to be shown above the markers' butt saying what the result was.

It takes very good shooting to hit the Running Man through the heart. If his carriage is well oiled, and gets a good shove off, he runs quite 12 miles an hour, a little faster as he descends into the dip, a little slower as he emerges. The open space that he has to cross in the middle between the two white posts is 25 yards, so that you have barely some four or five seconds in which to hit him. The range distance is 110 yards, so that a Lee-Enfield bullet with a 2000 feet per second muzzle velocity takes about 1-6th second to arrive there. Accordingly an allowance of about $2\frac{1}{2}$ feet ahead of the man has to be made in order that the bullet and the man may meet in their respective courses. It sounds all plain and simple enough, but let any rifleman try it after having been accustomed to a stationary target that will wait for him as long as he likes, and he is likely to find it not so easy as it looks.

Unfortunately, it is almost impossible to get any regular practice at a full-sized Running Man except at Bisley itself. It is a costly target to make, and a costly one to run, as may readily be imagined. But a safe and a useful substitute can be found by anyone who can command a good high wall or bank of earth as a stop-butt. The arrangement I adopt is very simple. It consists of two upright scaffold poles, 7 feet high, set firmly in the ground 10 feet apart with a crossbar on top, like a football goal. Behind the goal there are some sheds, a thick screen of bushes, and a high wall, which makes it perfectly safe. At Bisley the man starts from cover, so that he is already on the move when you catch sight of him. To imitate this there are a pair of empty barrels, 2 feet and 4 feet high respectively, which can be used to hide the points from which the targets start at either end, but in practice I find this too hard for the boys. Between the uprights two stout galvanised wires are strained by means of a key that turns the ratchet wheels in the strainers. These wire strainers can be bought for a few pence at any ironmonger's shop. The two wires slope a little in order that the target may run along them by gravity, and the slopes are in opposite directions; the angle is given by fastening the strainer to the post 5 or 6 inches higher at one end than at the other. Of course, the steeper the slope of the wire the speedier the run.

Each wire has its own target, consisting of a wooden box 15 inches by 10 by 5, filled with paper or shavings, and having a cardboard front. To the upper 5-inch side of the target are screwed two pulleys truly in line and exactly in the middle; these are to run on the wire and

PLATE XIV

The Running-Man Range in the Author's Garden

carry the target. The wheels of the pulleys should have
deep grooves that fit easily over the wire, and if you
cannot find pulleys in the shop that have one side open, so
as to hook on and off the wire, you had better get the
ironmonger to file a cut in one side of the cheek of the
pulleys (as shown in the illus-
tration) to admit the wire freely.

Having got your target,
hang it by its pair of pulleys
on one of the wires at the higher
end, and let it go; it will run,
steadily gaining speed, till it
bumps against the opposite post.
If you let wood bump on wood
the box will soon shatter itself.
I make a pad of leather nailed

to the post, and stuffed with old tennis balls cut
up, or any other scraps of elastic stuff. The pad may
be observed in Plate XIV., directly under the strainer.
A simple form of catch released by a lanyard suffices to
hold the target at the top of the slope ready to run when
asked.

For the figure of the Running Man himself I have
two plans. One is to paint a black figure on a sheet of
white paper representing a man about 4 inches high,
carrying a rifle, and to paste this on the cardboard face of
the target. All the beginners are put to shoot at this, and
they seem to find it a hard enough task to score upon it.
But the white background, which thus travels with the
figure, makes him a far easier mark than is offered by the
Bisley man of khaki hue with no background except
earth and bushes. So to get something nearer the Bisley
effect I suspend a khaki figure of cardboard below the

target, and with the bank of earth and bushes forming
the background I find my khaki man quite a sufficiently
hard nut to crack. With a B.S.A. air-rifle at 15 yards I
try to allow about an inch and a half, but everybody
must find out for himself the exact amount he needs.

I was out after rabbits one day with a young friend,
who did not succeed in hitting very many. He turned
to the keeper, who was shooting with us, and had showed
himself as deadly on a rabbit as most keepers are.

" James," said my young friend, " how far ahead of
your rabbit do you aim when you shoot ? "

The keeper looked at him severely. " Sir," he said,
" I allus haims straight at the hobject."

And that is what many good shots will tell you,
because that is the impression left on the firer's own mind
in snapshooting.   Nevertheless it is a perfectly well-
established fact that when a shot hits an object moving
across the line of fire, the barrel was most surely pointing
ahead of the object at the moment of release. If you
doubt this you had better experiment till you have satisfied yourself.

Now, let us suppose that I am at the firing point with
a beginner. I slip the string loop at the end of the
lanyard over my right foot, and take my position so that
it is just taut. I myself stand with the rifle below my
elbow, as at Bisley, but I tell the pupil to raise his to
the ready, and when the man appears to aim on the white
paper at least 3 or 4 inches in front of him. The pupil
gives the word " All right," I move the foot with the loop
a few inches back, and the lanyard pulls the pin, the
target emerges from behind the screen, if we are using
the screen, we fire as it crosses, and it vanishes behind the
other screen. The man is only in sight for about two

seconds, so that one has to take an even quicker aim than at Bisley.

If my pupil misses his man but gets on the target he can tell what he has done by the hole in the white paper. But shooting at the khaki man below the target I cannot tell after a miss whether I was too soon or too late, except by remembering just how the sights looked when I fired. One must trust to one's memory in the matter, and the same is the case at Bisley, for although there you see the bullet make a splash of sand on the face of the stop-butt, yet as the figure has gone on moving while the bullet was making the splash the impression left on the eye is that the shot had struck behind it, an impression which as often as not is purely an illusion.

And here again arises the great debate whether one should shoot with both eyes open or only one. It is certain that the majority of good shots with the fowling piece keep both eyes open, and it is a fair corollary from this that the same thing would hold good of men who shoot at a moving object with a rifle. I myself learned to close the left eye in shooting when young, and I find it difficult to get out of the habit entirely ; however, I am satisfied that I can do better with both eyes open at the Running Man, and the same appears to be the case with me at a fixed target whenever the light is very bad. Certainly in a bad light the left eye helps one to see the object very much more clearly and easily. I should advise every beginner, at least, to give two-eyed shooting a good trial.

Now, as to the way to take the allowance you desire to make on the man ; you can choose between swinging and snapping. If you swing the rifle, starting behind and gradually overtaking the moving object, you can fire whenever you think the allowance is just right. In short, you may be said to follow the object, only you follow in front. If you prefer to snap, you must bring the rifle into the path of the object, well ahead of it, and fire at the critical moment. I do not like this plan at all. If you delay for a moment, the time has gone by, you are late, and you know it; you check your finger, you don't pull, the man has gone, you start to follow him from behind, you get too far in front, only to find that the lost chance cannot be regained. No doubt with perfect nerve and perfect timing, very pretty practice may be made by snapping, but I can only repeat the advice of all shot-gun experts, viz., to cultivate " swing." Above all things, avoid pointing at a point in front of the moving object, hoping to get off the shot when it arrives. In one of his stories, Fenimore Cooper makes his " Path-finder " or " Deerslayer " " string " a brace of wheeling seagulls with a single bullet for the benefit of the heroine; nor would anyone who has seen a fine shot at work question the actual possibility of such a feat. But it takes genius, and genius is rare. At present I am thinking of the ordinary man who wants to make himself into a useful shot, and for him much the safest plan is to swing the sights steadily ahead of the moving target and time the right moment for releasing the trigger to the best of his power as he swings.

The Running Man at Bisley being khaki colour, and the background a sandy bank with bushes on it, it is hard to catch an ordinary black fore-sight quick enough. In the Far West when hunting game most hunters use a white ivory sight, and the same is true elsewhere. Circumstances vary, and if one was after a bear in snow, the white sight would probably be less satisfactory than a black, but generally the white fore-sight is better. I certainly prefer it myself. However, for beginners where you want the thing to be as easy as possible, make your target a black man on a white ground, and let them use the blackened sight.

In giving a first lesson to a beginner you will find it a good plan to put a black spot the size of a shilling some inches in front of the man; when the learner holds straight on the spot he hits the man, and sees the necessity of the allowance being taken with uniform accuracy. From this he can work his way on gradually. When he can hit the black man with tolerable accuracy it is time to try the effect of a less distinct figure on the target. If you paste dark brown wrapping paper on the target, and cut out a yellowish brown figure for him to shoot at he will find it much harder to hit, and can thus be led on to the khaki man with a natural background.

Some men find the deer at Bisley easier than the man as he is longer horizontally though shorter vertically. But in the matter of scoring the horizontal length is not an advantage. In real life if you want to eat an animal after you have shot it, you should lodge your bullet only in the head, neck, shoulders, or heart. If you hit him far back, he simply goes off wounded, and it may take you hours to get him, even if you don't lose him altogether, and when you have got him you probably find the best parts of the meat spoiled by the wound having allowed the blood and the fluid contents of the intestines to spread all about the haunch. So a shot in the after part of the deer used to be reckoned against you, not as a mere miss, but as a " haunch " shot, and the range officer at the firing point turned to you with a gentle smile of commiseration and remarked, " I am afraid that will cost you half-a-crown." The fine acted as a useful reminder to you not to be slow on the trigger again. However in 1906 the fine was abolished, for it obviously had the effect of discouraging men from trying their hand at the Deer. But though you are no longer fined, do not forget to hold well in front.

The boys who come to shoot in my garden enjoy themselves very well at the fixed targets, whether standing, sitting, or lying. Also I notice that shooting off the horse is exceedingly popular, and he is seldom without a rider. But if I put it to the vote, " Shall we go to the Running Man? " the answer is generally an enthusiastic affirmative. Variety is charming. As Voltaire declared of Education : " Toute methode est bonne fors l'ennuyeuse," and we turn with a natural sense of pleasure to each fresh form of our sport.

CHAPTER IX.

Shooting from Horseback.

To shoot off a horse is an art by itself, an art always difficult and sometimes dangerous. In my cowboy days our favourite Indian fighter on the frontier was General Custer. In the great war he had won quick promotion, and became general when he was only 24; he was a rider and a sportsman, but he had never been out in the Wild West, and had never run buffalo. So when he came out on the Plains he made up his mind to kill his first buffalo alone and unaided. He took his favourite thoroughbred charger and a .44 calibre Colt's pistol, and left his camp. After a long ride he found a herd of buffalo, got as near as he could unseen, and then, coming into view, started after them full speed. The buffalo scattered; Custer chose a mighty bull whose horns he coveted for a trophy, and pressed after him; the noble horse carried him up to the quarry. Custer drew his pistol, fired, and found himself hurled headlong to the ground. He had shot his own steed through the head.

It seems incredible that such a man as Custer could have done this, but, as a matter of fact, to kill your own horse instead of the buffalo was one of the commonest

results of a first attempt at buffalo running. When we
see Colonel Cody, known to us all as Buffalo Bill, breaking
glass balls tossed up while he gallops round the arena in
his Wild West Show, shooting from the saddle looks as
easy as shooting from an armchair; in reality it is the
exact contrary. In the old days there were many men
on the frontier who were skilled at it simply because they
had to be, and they learnt in what one might call the
natural way; they got on a steady horse, and fired off
his back with rifle and pistol till they could hit their
mark with fair certainty. Such an education was possible
enough in a country where you could buy a good pony
for £10, and where you could use as much of the bound-
less prairie as you liked for a practising ground. Here in
our crowded England, where it costs considerably more
than £20 merely to feed a horse for a year, and where
you have, quite properly, no right to go firing off guns
and pistols along the high road or over common land, and
where few farmers would welcome your doing so over their
fields, it is very hard to learn horseback shooting at all.

But something has been done in spite of these difficul-
ties. A riding machine has been invented which shakes
up the rider very much in the way that a horse does, and
gives him all he wants to do to make a good target from
its saddle. This curious steed is well shown in Plate XV.
It will be seen that it consists of a barrel-shaped body
suspended fore and aft by ropes from a frame in a way
that allows it to oscillate very considerably to either side,
and to a lesser extent back and forwards. The frame is
mounted on two large rockers of different curve, and when
either the rider himself or a friend sets the steed in
motion the rockers transmit to the barrel a curious rolling
gait as well as an up and down one that is singularly like

a horse's. An ordinary saddle is girthed on the barrel, and it will be noticed in Plate XV. that a horn like that of a cowboy saddle is affixed to the front of the barrel itself. This is not quite the correct position for a saddle-horn, but it does well enough for the lasso work which we also do with it, and the lasso itself may be seen hanging over the horn in the Frontispiece.

The " very fearful wildfowl " that appears ready to spring upon the rider in Plate XV. is really a monster made from the stump of an apple-tree and from some of the boughs that yielded natural knees, or rather hocks. He is an excellent dummy to throw the lasso at, but we do not shoot at him with the rifle, as, of course, the slugs would fly all about. For practice we use the same sort of box stop-butt as for ordinary air-rifle work, but I take care to have a good large one, seeing that the chances of a shot going wild are much greater. Also I like to use a larger target; a one-inch bull at six yards is hardly too much, so difficult is the quick aim to catch.

To judge how difficult it is one must get into the saddle with an air-rifle and try to hold it on the bull. A beginner will probably find it a hard task to keep the sights bearing within six inches of the bull during a single " stride " of the horse. You will find that during the swing your sights travel both sideways and up and down in a way that is very puzzling; they never stop moving for a moment, so that it is quite impossible to dwell on the shot. You have to watch the bull, and when you see the sights coming to the bull, release the trigger with a firm, swift pressure. The thing is hard to describe; you have to observe and so teach yourself. I think it is a very great help to keep both eyes open, but whether you use one eye or two the great problem is how to time your

shot properly. Make up your mind with decision that
you have got to get the knack, though at first you will
be dismayed and astonished to find how many wild shots
you put in ; very likely you will not be able to average
better than outers, say 14 for 7 shots. And those are
outers scored upon a target that is four times larger than
it would be if you were lying down to it. After a little
while you will probably be able to average magpies, or
21 for 7. Perhaps you may reach a stage where you will
average inners, 28 for 7, at least on your good days. And
if you are a genius you may go higher yet ; the best score
I have seen was 14 consecutive shots which realised 63
out of 70.

For the expert who can make inners at a stationary
mark I have devised a pendulum target, which swings to
and fro at the end of the gallery, suspended by two cords.
When the horse and the target are both in full swing it
is uncommonly hard to average better than outers.

Let me repeat, for there is not much more to be said
by way of advice, that the great thing is to catch the
knack, and this can only be attained by frequent and by
earnest, strongly-purposed practice. As soon as you can
do the trick at all on the fixed target, you may find it
fairly easy to score magpies there ; but you will hardly
improve on that unless you make the greatest effort to
concentrate your attention during that critical fraction of
a second when the sights are moving towards the bull.
To be neither too soon nor too late, to restrain the eager
finger till the right moment, to be quick on the trigger
when it comes—these are the cardinal points.

A patent for the mechanical horse has been taken out,
and it is hoped that the invention may be put upon the
market ere long at a reasonable price. The horse shown

in Plate XV. stands about 14 hands, but, of course, one could be built to any height. Ordinarily the horse lives in a corner of my glass shooting gallery, where he takes up a space of about 8 feet by 4. If I used him much upon the lawn I should have to put boards underneath the rockers to keep them from cutting in. The heavy rockers make it practically impossible to overset him, but the rope slings allow the barrel to turn half over sideways, so that in mounting it is necessary to go up lightly with a spring, otherwise you pull your mount over to you unpleasantly. Getting on like this affords excellent practice for mounting the back of a real horse.

How far this mechanical horse trains a man to shoot from a live animal it is hard to say precisely. I should say it did a great deal to start him in the right way. Although, of course, the motion cannot be quite the same as that of a real horse, it is sufficiently near it to make the aiming very similar. Good timing and quickness are of the essence of shooting from a moving seat, and they are things it is all-important to acquire before you take the field. It is a poor time to start to learn them when you are being vigorously prodded with a spear by an active enemy.

When our forces defeated the Mad Mullah's Dervish army at Jidballi, some Somali native levies whom we had armed with rifles and mounted on horses were sent in pursuit of the scattered and retreating Dervishes; but when they caught them up they were absolutely unable to do them much harm, for not having been trained, they could not hit them from the back of a horse even at five yards. The Somalis would have had to put the muzzle almost against their man to hit him, but they wisely abstained from getting to such close quarters, for the

Dervish spearman with his shovel-headed spear was an awkward customer if you went within thrusting distance. If these raw mounted riflemen had had time, perhaps, they would have learned how to shoot on horseback. Our own soldiers in South Africa had, some of them at least, learned by 1902 ; but it was a sadly expensive school that educated them.

My mechanical horse needs no guiding and wears no bridle, so that one can shoot comfortably with both hands free. On a live horse one must drop the reins while shooting, and if there is any guiding to be done the rider has to manage that with the pressure of his legs, for which purpose the steed must be thoroughly well trained. Where the horse has not been trained to this, and it becomes imperative to shoot from the saddle, the best if not the only plan is to guide with one hand and shoot with the other. I have a boy's light air-gun weighing only 4lb., which may be seen in the frontispiece, where the rider is aiming backwards, and with this I have seen targets made one-handed, scoring outers or perhaps a trifle better. But it is a very unsatisfactory plan at best, and if one were holding a heavy rifle weighing nine or ten pounds in one hand I should say it was almost hopeless. On the only occasion when I have seen one-handed shooting in actual practice it was done with a 7lb. Winchester carbine. I was out prospecting with Garcia, my Mexican companion, in Piedra Park, in the San Juan mountains, when we suddenly ran on to a grizzly bear at about 50 yards distance. I was riding a pet mule, Captain Jinks, a very small and very scary animal ; I took a hasty shot from the saddle, and either missed the bear or only touched him up slightly. But at the shot he turned and ran like a scared wolf, and we after him. The

PLATE XV

Realism is achieved by reproducing natural conditions for the cultivation of snap-shooting

country was splendid for riding, as open as an English park, but for all I could do with a pair of Spanish spurs I could not persuade the timid little mule to close on him. The Mexican, however, was mounted on a gallant, Mormon-bred stallion, who with fine courage took him right up alongside the bear. But the man though a splendid rider was no great shot, and it made me laugh as I pounded along behind to see him raise the carbine again and again in his right hand, bring it down like a pistol, and bang away at Bruin. Every time he shot, the alarmed bear fairly humped himself to escape, until after a good run of about five furlongs we found ourselves at the end of the park and at the base of a rugged mountain covered with thick scrub in which Br'er B'ar promptly disappeared.

No; if you must shoot one-handed from the saddle, a pistol is infinitely preferable. I have an air pistol weighing 2lb. which shoots a No. 1 slug, and I have seen scores of 20 out of 35 made with it off the horse, though it is as a weapon considerably less accurate than any of my air-guns or air-rifles. The art of aiming it is similar to that necessary with the rifle, only that if possible one must be even quicker on the trigger. And in this an ounce of practice is worth a pound of theory.

CHAPTER X.

Orthoptic and
Telescopic Sights.

So far we have dealt only with the ordinary open sight, but for really close shooting at long ranges most men prefer a more elaborate arrangement. The form which this most commonly takes is what is called here an "orthoptic," but in the Far West was known as a "peep" sight. In this the back-sight is a pin-hole in a thin steel plate which rises from the stock of the rifle just in front of the right eye, when the cheek rests on the butt in aiming. When you look through the pinhole you see a surprisingly large circular view of the landscape; and after being accustomed to the narrow V notch you are inclined to believe that to take an accurate aim with such a large field is out of the question. But it is not so, for if the elevation of the orthoptic sight has been correctly adjusted, then when you see the top of the fore-sight in the middle of your circular view straight under the bull you will find the bullet will go true to the mark.

It is quite feasible to use the ordinary barley-corn fore-sight, but it is far better to have what the

Americans call a globe-sight; this is a small round steel
bead, on top of a pin, which stands up in a little steel
tunnel over the barrel, and is thus shaded from the light
and protected from injury.   Seen through
the pinhole it appears as in the illustration.   These   sights   can   be   employed
with   excellent   effect   in   hunting,   provided that there is a good light and that
your game is standing still.   When I was
ranching thirty years ago, many hunters used
them for killing antelope on the Great Plains; I myself
had them fitted on a Sharpe's .50 calibre for that purpose.   However, in a dull light it is unquestionably harder
to see with them than with open sights, and few hunters
can manage a running shot with the orthoptic.   To meet
this difficulty there is a very neat combination, called the
Lyman fore-sight, which is hinged on its base.   Turn it
up, and you have a globe-sight precisely as figured above;
turn it down, and the other part stands up like an
ordinary fore-sight, and you can fold down the pinhole

Peephole Back-sight as fitted to; B.S.A.' Air-Rifle.

back-sight and use the V back-sight on the barrel.   I found this a thoroughly practical arrangement.

In the American Civil War there were a few wise generals who selected a small number of really crack shots as sharpshooters, and allowed them to use any sort of rifle and any form of sights they liked; they were given a horse to ride and an orderly to carry all the extra fixings they wanted.   These marksmen were kept in cotton wool, so to speak, and when need arose they were put into chosen positions where every shot would tell; their murderous fire sometimes had a surprising effect on a battle.   The ordinary soldier, however, strongly resented the idea of being deliberately potted in this way, and it was a maxim with him that no quarter should be given to any man who carried " fancy sights " on his rifle.   But that was more than forty years ago, and I dare say we have changed all that.

Those American generals realised what is unknown to many of our people still—the extraordinary effect that may sometimes be produced by a single marksman under certain circumstances.   When Kitchener attempted right at the start to rush Cronje's laager at Paardeburg by a vigorous general attack, a young officer who happened to be a Bisley shot found himself temporarily in the company of a regiment that had been ordered along with some more to advance up the line of the Modder.   Before them lay a terrible half-mile of the bare African veldt swept by a desolating Mauser fire.   They had been heavily punished, and the survivors were lying under what cover they could find behind anthills.   An infernal pompom was playing upon them here, and they were firing vainly back at it without checking its fire in the least, for they neither knew the range nor even exactly where it was. The Bisley

PLATE XVI

Shooting with the Service Rifle in the Back Position

man crawled around among our dead, and gathered to
himself a Lee-Enfield and a goodly supply of cartridges ;
then he chose a position behind a convenient ant-hill,
whence he carefully examined the Boer entrenchments,
and presently he spotted a good-sized patch of whitish
sand close to where he guessed that hateful pompom was
concealed. He took the patch of sand for his target, and
fired shot after shot at it, altering his sight every time
and watching for the splash of his bullet after each shot,
until, after trying a variety of elevations, he saw the sand
fly up. He fired a few more shots to make sure, for with
the confusion of a battle going on any particular bullet-
splash might have come from anywhere. But when he
saw the sand splash every time he fired he was thoroughly
satisfied that at last he had got the true elevation. Then
he turned his rifle on the place where he guessed that the
pompom was, and put about a hundred shots into the
embrasure. Apparently he had touched the spot ; the
pompom ceased fire and was taken away somewhere else,
and the regiment was released from a bad fix.

There are people who sneer at the Bisley man, but he
can do something sometimes if he gets a chance.

However, this little bit of service was performed
without the aid of orthoptic sights, though probably the
Bisley man would have been glad enough of them had
he found them on the dead man's Lee-Enfield. But he
might have had an orthoptic in his pocket ; in the place
of having your pinhole back-sight attached to the rifle it
is possible to use a pair of spectacles of which the
left eye is either quite open or of clear or slightly-tinted
glass, while before the right is a dark plate with a pinhole in it. In this case the ordinary back-sight is used
for the aim, which must be taken by looking at it through

the pinhole; the effect of the orthoptic spectacles is to give a much sharper definition to both the back-sight and the fore-sight. Young eyes do not need this help so much, but in later life, when the lenses of the eye flatten, the orthoptic becomes as useful as a crutch is to a lame man. And when the eye is actually defective to start with, or has become so with age, a little lens can be inserted in the orthoptic to correct the fault of the organ. I always have one air-gun fitted with an orthoptic sight by means of which I can try a boy's eyes if he shoots inexplicably badly with open sights, and faults have been revealed in this way which called for the aid of the oculist. This has happened more than once, and that, too, in the case of schoolboys whose teachers had never suspected there was anything wrong. A boy's eyes may be good enough for reading books, but the test of shooting with them soon discloses any weakness. It is worth while having a boy taught to shoot merely to know that his eyes are all right.

Orthoptic sights fitted to the rifle are barred in ordinary " Service rifle " competitions, but the competitor is now permitted to wear orthoptic spectacles or to use a peephole bored in a metal plate attached below the brim of his hat. There have been some military weapons brought out by inventors in which an aperture back-sight has been fitted on the barrel almost as far forward as the ordinary sight. Being so far from the eye the aperture has to be much larger than a pinhole; I do not myself find that, when the lens of an eye has flattened with advancing years, such an aperture helps in the very least, and it seems to interfere with taking a quick aim for snapshooting. However, time will show if it is an improvement.

For actual work at game, the bead form of fore-sight shown on page 81 is suitable.   But for target work many

men prefer another, where there is a little ring instead and the sight can be brought on to the target so that the ring encircles the bull, giving you perfect definition.   I have never tried the

ring on game, but for match-rifle shooting it is considered indispensable, and the majority of match-rifle owners provide themselves with both the ring and the bead, made so as to be interchangeable.   I have an air-gun with the ring fore-sight and the elevating aperture sight on the stock that I managed to put on myself.

Match-rifle shooting is largely done at extreme ranges of 1000 to 1200 yards.   The men who go in for it often shoot lying on their backs, and have their orthoptic backsight fitted at the very heel of the rifle-butt so as to bring it closer to the eye, as may be seen on the B.S.A. air-rifle in Plate XIII.

A pair of orthoptic spectacles will cost some 10s. or 12s., and in choosing them most men prefer to get those that have a little steel tube that projects from the front of the plate, only the line of projection is not quite straight forward, but turns slightly askew towards the bridge of the nose.   When a man takes aim with a rifle he looks out of the inner corner of his eye so that the skew tube points just the way he wants ; the tube is fitted with a revolving front, pierced with five pinholes, of different sizes, any one of which you can use according to the light.   Some are fitted with a contracting iris diaphragm instead of five varying holes.   Both forms are good.

The telescopic sight I have never had fitted to an air-gun, though a friend of mine has done so with complete success. The telescope is attached above the barrel and parallel with it, and adjusted by screws so that it lies in the same vertical plane. On looking through the eye-piece you see the object magnified, and you also see two or more cross-wires like those of an astronomical glass, as in the illustration herewith. Place the intersection of the wires on the object, and the bullet should hit it. The telescopic sight can be used for game. Jim Hamlin, or Rebel Jim as he was called, sent in 300 antelope to Colorado Springs in the single month of September, 1874, from the ranges beyond my ranch; they were all killed with his telescopic rifle, and I fancy it was a record number at the time. But it is obvious that a weapon so fitted is bound to be somewhat delicate as well as decidedly expensive, and I do not think any armies have so far thought of adopting it for wear and tear work. But it is used for cannon both in the army and navy.

At Bisley telescopic glasses are freely used in combination with the match-rifle sights, which are employed for the long ranges, but in the ordinary run of competitions they are barred. In fact at Bisley, as well as at most other full-range meetings, the conditions for the great majority of the shoots are "Service rifle," and in these all fancy sights on the rifle are barred as well as telescopes. And this is quite as it should be, for the object is to interest the mass of men, be they private soldiers, volunteers, or yeomanry, in making themselves effective shots. A telescopic sight must comprise in the first instance a telescope of the highest quality. It must be constructed to a special design, and it is not therefore surprising that it can easily cost more than the rifle to which it is fitted.   Nevertheless, it would be a good thing if everybody knew how to use a telescopic sight, and incidentally it would have the advantage of getting men practically accustomed to the use of a telescope.   A man has to learn to focus it, to point it so as to find what he wishes to examine, and to adjust his own eye so as to see through it properly.   All this sounds as easy as A B C, but it takes a bit of learning, and it is a pity to wait to begin till you are sent out on scout against an alert enemy.

One hint may be given to anyone who gets a chance to try a friend's telescopically-sighted rifle for the first time.   If it is fired with a full charge the recoil may drive the eyepiece back so as to inflict a blow on the eye.   To prevent this it is usual to have a cup of black rubber at the eyepiece end so that the eye is held at a safe distance to the rear.   But if you had a telescopic sight fitted to a B.S.A. air-rifle the absence of recoil would render this precaution unnecessary.   The most modern telescopes are made so that the natural position for the eye is some three inches or so from the object glass, thereby obviating all danger of a bruised eye.

Doubtless the future has in store for us yet higher developments in the art of shooting than telescopic sights, but it would puzzle a prophet to guess what they will be. Meantime to master what we have already is enough.   And I would say this to the men who are conscious that advancing years are making them too old for active service :—You may still find pleasure in handing on to a younger generation the knowledge of arms.   It does an old heart good to see how eager the youths grow, and to watch the self-respect and self-control that the sense of mastery brings out in them. They can be exercised effectively in all the various forms of the gunner's art even in a garden, and by the time your recruit has learned to shoot standing, sitting, or lying down, to use both the point-blank and long-range sights, to take snapshots at the disappearing man, to hit the running mark as well as the stationary target, and to shoot from horseback as well as on the ground, he has fairly earned the title of the complete air-gunner.

THE "B.S.A." AIR RIFLE.

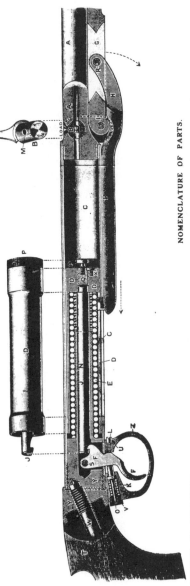

METHOD OF OPERATION.

Compressing the Spring.—The rifle is set ready for shooting by freeing from its retaining catch the hand-lever G, and pressing it in the direction marked by the dotted arrow. Through the medium of the link H the movement of the lever on its pivot I is transmitted to the piston D, which is thereby thrust backwards against the powerful resistance of the piston spring E. The backward movement is continued until the trigger F hooks into the piston rod J. The trigger adjustment screw L serves to regulate the pull-off of the trigger.

Inserting the Pellet.—The pellet is inserted by giving a quarter turn to the lever of the breech plug B. This plug contains a hole M, and, according to the position of the lever, the hole lies in a continuous line with the barrel, or at right angles with the same. To load the rifle, the lever is turned to the vertical position, and a pellet is inserted through the hole marked LOAD. The lever is then turned down, and the slug lies in the barrel ready for discharge.

NOMENCLATURE OF PARTS.

A	Barrel.	R	Link Axis Screw.
B	Breech Plug.	S	Trigger Axis Screw.
C	Cylinder.	T	Butt or Stock.
D	Piston.	U	Trigger Adjustment Locking Screw.
E	Piston Spring.	V	Trigger Plunger Screw.
F	Trigger.	W	Stock Bolt.
G	Hand Lever.	X	Piston Rod Keeper Screw.
H	Link.	Y	Trigger Block.
I	Lever Axis Screw.	Z	Guard.
J	Piston Rod.		
K	Trigger Spring.		
L	Trigger Adjustment Screw.		
M	Hole in Breech Plug.		
	(not strictly a part).		
N	Piston Rod Guide Tube.		
O	Trigger Plunger.		
P	Leather Washer.		
Q	Leather Washer Screw.		

PARTS NOT SHOWN OR LETTERED.

Lever Catch Block.	Breech Plate Screws (2).
Stock Bolt Washer.	Guard Side Screw.
Sight Spring.	Butt Plate Screws (2).
Lever Catch Spring.	Keeper Screws for Link and Lever Axis Screws (2).
Breech Plug Spring.	Trigger Block Peg.
Sight Adjustment Screw.	Lever Catch Pin.
Breech Plug Plate.	
Butt Plate.	
Front Sight.	
Back Sight Bed.	
Back Sight Leaf.	
Lever Catch.	

RIFLE CASES.

WICKER AND CANE. (Registered Designs.)
Suitable for Miniature and Air Rifles.

No. 1. Registered No. 495060.
BEST BUFF WICKER, LINED WATERPROOF. **16/-** each.

No. 2. Registered No. 495059.
BEST BUFF WICKER, LINED WATERPROOF. **14/6** each.

No. 3. BEST QUALITY REED CANE, VARNISHED OAK COLOUR,
LINED WATERPROOF. **9/3** each.

LIGHT, STRONG and WATERPROOF.

*To be obtained from Gun and Cycle Dealers,
or direct from the Manufacturers* . . . .

JOHN J. PLATER & SONS,

262, 263 & 264, Bradford St. **BIRMINGHAM.**
and Green Street,
'Phone: 1169 Central. *Telegrams: Wicker, Birmingham.*

London Office and Showroom:
34, PATERNOSTER ROW, E.C. 'Phone: 1473 Central.

AIR-RIFLES.

No matter how extensive an armoury the enthusiastic shooter may possess, he will probably obtain more regular enjoyment and more positive pleasure from the casual use of his air-rifle than from all the other arms put together. To the man who must live within easy reach of his daily work, the air-rifle is the only weapon with which regular practice can be obtained without going outside the limits of an ordinary suburban garden.

Great as were the mechanical problems to be overcome in designing and manufacturing a satisfactory air-rifle, the problems in question have been absolutely solved in the B.S.A. model. Its use is accordingly unhesitatingly recommended to those who have in the past stood aloof from air-guns on account of their reputation for frequently needing repair and their hitherto incurable lack of accuracy.

SEND FOR PRINTED MATTER.

The Birmingham Small Arms Co., Ltd.,

BIRMINGHAM.

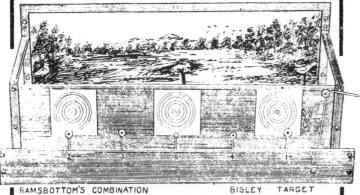

B.S.A. Military Air-Rifle

(See Plates in body of this Work).

PRICE 80/- EACH.

The weight, balance, and sights are the same as those of the ·303 Long Lee-Enfield Service Rifle.

The Military Air Rifle possesses the same general "feel" as the Service Rifle, and is used in many Drill Halls for instructing recruits in the art of shooting. It is also found invaluable by efficient marksmen as a means of maintaining their skill during the winter months at a minimum of expense.

Comparing the Air Rifle with other methods of giving miniature range practice, its purchase may be recommended as a sound commercial speculation, in that the original cost is covered by the saving effected in the first 7000 rounds used. That is to say, a B.S.A. Military Air Rifle and 7000 rounds of ammunition cost about the same sum of money as 7000 rounds of ordinary ·22 ammunition alone, or 3000 rounds of Morris Tube ammunition.

The rifle is used by many regiments, including
The Royal Horse Guards.
The 1st V.B. Royal Warwickshire Regt.
The Central London Rangers.

Sole Manufacturers . .

THE BIRMINGHAM SMALL ARMS CO., LTD.,
BIRMINGHAM.

ELEY
CARTRIDGES.

"SPORTING"

"MILITARY"

"CLUB SHOOTING"

AIR-GUN SLUGS.

TO BE HAD OF ALL

GUNMAKERS & DEALERS

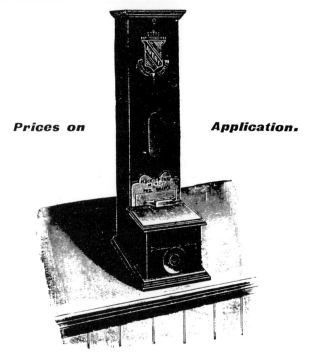